Discipline By Subtraction

The Art of Strategic Laziness

James R. Snoddy

Cover design by Habiba Babar
Copy editing by Amy Jane Harris

Printed in the United States of America

ISBN: 979-8-9994727-2-4
First edition
Published by Madder Lion Press

For Nadia and Alessandro, the two loves of my life.

Table of Contents

Introduction

Reclaiming lost bandwidth can be the difference between just surviving and thriving. As an Army infantry officer, diplomat, entrepreneur, husband, and father with a high operational tempo, I've learned to identify and optimize the hidden moments—the bandwidth—that others overlook. This book teaches how to do that in a deliberate, measurable, and sustainable way.

Scarcity taxes our minds. When bandwidth is low, IQ drops, patience thins, and mistakes multiply. Subtraction isn't about minimalism; it's about reclaiming the mental RAM you're already paying for.[1]

Whether you're a parent, a policymaker, or a platoon leader, this book will show you how to reclaim time, cut unnecessary effort, and live smarter, without sacrificing excellence.

Whereas others tell you to do less, this book shows you how to systematically subtract the waste and measure the payoff, which allows you to do more.

This philosophy stands on the massive shoulders of Peter Drucker, Greg McKeown, Tim Ferriss, and James Clear, all profoundly effective time managers.

Where they proposed principles, we build systems. Where they inspired, we operationalize.

---

[1] Sendhil Mullainathan & Eldar Shafir, *Scarcity: Why Having Too Little Means So Much.* (New York: Times Books, 2013.)

The Subtracted Symbol

This is not a logo. It's a signal.

The red bar is a subtracted symbol that used to be addition, but it's not math. It's a doctrine and a discipline. It is strategy over struggle.

It appears on the cover as the quiet standard for those who build systems that don't require applause. It's a symbol for people who:

- Refuse ceremony
- Kill sacred cows
- Design around failure
- Respect time as capital

The bar is red because subtraction hurts. Not everyone can do it. Subtraction demands clarity. It forces you to name what doesn't serve you and straight up delete it. Not someday. Not tomorrow. Now. Right now. It's not just about doing less. It's about doing less on purpose, with results that compound when no one's watching.

A Glyph for the Already Efficient

This book wasn't written for the scattered or the stuck. It was written for you—the competent, the overleveraged, the silently burning. The red bar is for you.

1. You don't need more apps.
2. You need fewer obligations.
3. You don't need more energy.
4. You need less friction.
5. You don't need more motivation.
6. You need systems that subtract without asking.

This bar won't make you better. But if you carry it forward, it might make everything else easier.

Foreword: The Art of Strategic Laziness

This book is not for everyone. It is not for the disorganized. It's not for the people looking for another motivational quote or a shortcut to feel productive. This is not for people looking for an attaboy. It's for the overachievers. The overloaded. The ones already sprinting and wondering why they still can't catch up.

Strategic Laziness is the strategy of doing less, better. It's the doctrine of removing drag before adding speed. It's the rejection of performative discipline in favor of mission-aligned movement.

We do not stand on ceremony—we put our foot on its neck.

The core question is ruthless and simple: Does this thing we're doing gain us anything of value? If the answer is no, **then we do not do that thing**, and we reclaim the time, money, and clarity that others waste.

We do not inherit routines—we interrogate them.

I don't make my bed. I don't tie a tie more than once. I don't waste time on tasks that don't return value. Not just because I'm lazy, but because my time has a job.

We do not perform order—we design it.

This isn't a guide to becoming a robot. It's a blueprint for becoming deliberate.

You'll find tactics in here. Tools. Tables. ROI math. But more than anything, you'll find systems that are designed to make your life sharper, lighter, and better aligned with what matters.

Every chapter is built on three truths:
7. Time is a finite resource with a dollar value.
8. Many daily tasks are low-yield and fixable.
9. The clever and lazy, those who think hard and move smart, outperform the busy every time.

This is a field manual. A doctrine. An absolute rejection of hustle culture, checklist dopamine, and ceremonial productivity (remember: we put our foot on the neck of ceremony).

It's not for everyone. But if you've ever felt like the systems around you are bloated, broken, or slowing you down, welcome. You're not the problem. Your bandwidth is. And this book teaches you how to subtract things from your life that produce unnecessary friction.

Subtraction Systems: A *Subtraction System* is a repeatable process that eliminates unnecessary effort, decisions, or friction without compromising the outcome. It's not a hack. It's a permanent deletion that increases bandwidth by removing low value drag from your life, enabling you to be Strategically Lazy.

Subtraction Feels Wrong, At First

Subtraction systems feel uncomfortable because they cut against identity: being responsive, busy, and self-reliant. Here's what might feel wrong, and why it's not:
10. Leaving your bed unmade makes you feel sloppy. But it buys you time.
11. Not replying instantly feels rude. But delayed replies are more focused.
12. Saying "no" to meetings feels risky. But you win back hours.
The discomfort eventually fades. But the ROI you regain does not.

Not everything worth doing has a measurable ROI. Some rituals bring joy; some frictions build resilience. This book doesn't advocate eliminating everything inefficient, only the inefficiencies you don't value. Subtraction is about reclaiming control. You don't cut what you love. You cut what clogs your system without meaning.

The Value of One Minute

If you can eliminate just one minute per day, you're not just saving time, you're multiplying bandwidth. The ROI of small efficiencies compounds in the same way money does: quietly, then completely (or, as Hemingway paraphrased: "gradually, then all at once," when discussing bankruptcy).

This table shows the long-term value of trimming even the smallest recurring tasks. Whether it's skipping one click, cutting one transition, or deleting one pointless notification, every minute counts.

Subtraction System	Days Per Year	Minutes Saved Daily	Hours Saved Yearly	Days Saved Lifetime	Annual Value	Lifetime Value
Kill 1-minute task	365	1	6.1	12.7	$305	$15,250
Kill 3-minute habit	365	3	18.3	38.1	$915	$45,750
Kill 5-minute friction point	260	5	21.7	45.2	$1,085	$54,250
Kill 10-minute sync	130	10	21.7	45.2	$1,085	$54,250
Kill 15-minute commute	130	15	32.6	67.8	$1,630	$81,500

ROI Assumption (Applies to All Tables): Unless otherwise stated, all ROI calculations assume a conservative time value of $50/hour, 130/260/365 days per year, and a 50-year outlook. These figures are meant to be illustrative, not prescriptive. All dollar figures in this book are for 2025 and future values do not include inflation. Obviously, if your hourly rate is not $50, you can readjust (I know you can do math; you wouldn't be reading this book otherwise).

Expected Inflation Multipliers (Based on 2.5% Average Annual Inflation):

Years	Multiplier	Interpretation
10	~1.28×	$1 today = ~$1.28 in 10 years
20	~1.64×	$1 today = ~$1.64 in 20 years
50	~3.39×	$1 today = ~$3.39 in 50 years

Time isn't the problem. Design is.

We think we're too busy. We think we're out of bandwidth. But the truth is simpler: we're wasting the time we already have.

This book isn't about doing more. It's about doing less, on purpose, with precision, and with systems that scale. Subtraction Systems are the foundation. Each one reclaims minutes, hours, and dollars. Stack them, and you get exponential returns.

All ROI figures in this book are scaled using **conservative assumptions**: modest daily use, a certain number of active days per year, and time valued at $50/hour, unless otherwise indicated. These aren't inflated numbers. They're deliberately modest to preempt skepticism and to reflect what a busy, inconsistent human can achieve. If anything, your actual returns will exceed them.

And here's the kicker: you don't have to perform these systems every day. You don't need perfection. If you run any Subtraction System **just half the time**, you'll still see massive gains. This is the real adoption model: friction-aware, self-reinforcing, and designed to survive real life. Apply one. Then another. You already have the time and the money. Now it's time to reclaim them.

What if Everyone Did it?

If every person on Earth saved just 15 minutes per day, we'd reclaim **83.3 million years—every year**. That's the time from now back to the Late Cretaceous, when dinosaurs still roamed. It's not a metaphor. It's math. Subtraction scales. What does one minute matter? Everything—if it scales. Here's what happens when you subtract **just one minute** of waste per person, per day:

Size (population)	Minutes Saved Daily	Hours Saved Annually	Days Saved Lifetime	Annual Value	Lifetime Value
Human (1)	15	91	190	$4,563	$228,125
Family (4)	60	365	760	$18,250	$912,500
Classroom (25)	375	2,281	4,753	$114,063	$5,703,125
School (1,000)	15,000	91,250	190,104	$4,562,500	$228,125,000
Town (10,000)	150,000	912,500	1,901,042	$45,625,000	$2,281,250,000
City (100,000)	1,500,000	9,125,000	19,010,417	$456,250,000	$22,812,500,000
New York City (8,500,000)	127,500,000	775,625,000	1,615,885,417	$38,781,250,000	$1,939,062,500,000
California (39,000,000)	585,000,000	3,558,750,000	7,414,062,500	$177,937,500,000	$8,896,875,000,000
USA (331,000,000)	4,965,000,000	30,203,750,000	62,924,479,167	$1,510,187,500,000	$75,509,375,000,000
India (1,400,000,000)	21,000,000,000	127,750,000,000	266,145,833,333	$6,387,500,000,000	$319,375,000,000,000
World (8,000,000,000)	120,000,000,000	730,000,000,000	1,520,833,333,333	$36,500,000,000,000	$1,825,000,000,000,000

Now imagine every person on Earth saves just 15 minutes a day and uses it for real, substantive work, charity, or introspection. That's not a hard ask.

Author's Note: What This Is Not

None of this is about becoming cold or clinical with your human relationships. It's not about shaving off every moment until you're just a sapient calendar. It's about reclaiming your time so you can be more human, not less.

Every Subtraction System is designed to fulfill one goal: get the friction out of your way so you can show up where it matters. That means less time in checkout lines, inbox hell, or trying to find your keys, and more time with your kids, your partner, your purpose.

This book isn't about efficiency for its own sake. It's about reclaiming your bandwidth. And bandwidth is what lets you be present, generous, calm, and unhurried in a world that's constantly trying to steal your attention.

The ground truth here is the systems are what let me be human.

And that's the point.

Also, let's be clear: I'm not a world-class diplomat, soldier, or entrepreneur.

I've worked on defense, diplomacy, and policy challenges across five continents. I've led soldiers in combat, managed complex technology portfolios, negotiated cross-border frameworks, and contributed to high-stakes decisions at global forums. I've tackled restitution cases, consulted on national digital priorities, and helped bridge the cultural divide between strategists, operators, and technologists.

My career has stretched from jungle fieldwork to international conference rooms to selling Jeep hammocks at Daytona. But the friction is always the same: systems break, coordination drags, and time evaporates.

This book comes from those lived environments. It isn't academic. It's doctrine, forged under constraint. I've worn the uniforms, carried the briefcases, shipped the orders, and chased the deadlines—but the one thread that consistently mattered across combat, policy, parenting, and business was time management.

That's it.

I am an effective time manager.

I've learned how to reclaim bandwidth wherever I find it, stack wins across multiple domains and execute under pressure without coming unglued. You don't have to be brilliant to win. You just have to stop wasting your time.

That's what this book teaches. How to stop losing by default and start winning on purpose.

AI Acknowledgment

This book was authored by me with assistance from AI. The AI was used throughout the writing process as a structured thinking partner—for refining language, testing logic, clarifying structure, performing time/value modeling, data estimation, and ROI calculations. All original systems, frameworks, and insights originated from my thirty-plus years of personal experience. AI served as an accelerant to clarity and execution, not a substitute for authorship or judgment. And honestly, if I were to write *this* book on *this* topic without using AI, I would've violated the very principles the book teaches.

Doors and Corners

"I keep warning you. Doors and corners, kid. That's where they get you. Humans are too f*cking stupid to listen."

—Detective Josephus Aloisus Miller, *Abaddon's Gate,* by James S.A. Corey

Miller wasn't just talking about walls. He was talking about vulnerabilities, entry points and blind spots. The stuff you forget to guard. The same applies in life: friction doesn't storm the gates. It slips in through your calendar, inbox, and bad habits. A few unguarded meetings or errands, and the system starts leaking. Strategic Laziness locks the doors, pies the corners, and removes anything that clutters the path. The path to discipline isn't through addition; it's through judicious subtraction.

"Zakalwe, in all human societies we have ever reviewed, in every age and every state, there has seldom if ever been a shortage of eager young males prepared to kill and die to preserve the security, comfort and prejudices of their elders, and what you call heroism is just an expression of this simple fact; there is never a scarcity of idiots."

—Dziet Sma, Special Circumstances Officer, *Use of Weapons,* by Iain M. Banks

Sma isn't just commenting on war. She's commenting on habit. On repetition without reflection. On how easy it is to confuse familiar effort with meaningful impact. Whether it's warfare, meetings, or inbox triage, the pattern holds: people will spend their lives reenacting what feels heroic instead of asking what's effective. You can admire Zakalwe. But don't build your system like his. Systems don't get tired. They don't burn out. And they don't confuse motion for progress. That's why this quote is here. Not to warn you off war, but to warn you off grinding.

(Also, I love Iain M. Banks' *The Culture* series and James S.A. Corey's *The Expanse* series and wanted to honor them. Check them out!)

Mission Statement – Discipline by Subtraction: The Art of Strategic Laziness

This book is a field manual for recovering bandwidth: time, energy, and clarity, not by doing more, but by doing less, better. We call it Strategic Laziness: the disciplined subtraction of wasteful tasks, performative effort, and low-ROI habits in service of sharper outputs and cleaner systems.

The goal is to build Strategic Architects, people who structure their work and lives around intelligent constraints. Who reclaim hours not through hustle, but through deletion. Who build systems that render good choices automatic and bad habits obsolete.

What you reclaim isn't necessarily leisure; it's bandwidth. Space to move, think, and lead.

This is not minimalism. And it's not laziness. It's a discipline.

This is Discipline by Subtraction.

The Dehumidifier Doctrine: My Seminal Moment (MICRO)

This example isn't sexy. It won't save you a million bucks. But it is poignant and emblematic of the entire issue of building systems to recoup bandwidth.

When I was a kid, one of my least favorite chores was emptying the dehumidifier. I would shuffle to the basement, pull out that brown bucket, and dump moldy water into the utility sink. Twice a day. If I forgot, I got in trouble. One day, I noticed a small, threaded drain on the base of the drain bucket, still covered by a plug, and wondered if a hose leading to the sump pump might fix this problem forever. But I didn't act. Instead, I continued that endless cycle: lift, dump, replace. It was mindless, pointless, and worst of all: avoidable.

Decades later, when I was stationed in humid, tropical Trinidad and Tobago, I finally fixed it: I elevated the dehumidifier, ran a hose from the bucket, and drained it directly into a sink. That one-time, $4, 10-minute system saved hours over the following years and permanently killed a task I'd hated since childhood.

ROI Dehumidifier Doctrine (2x a Day)

Subtraction System	Minutes Saved Daily	Hours Saved Yearly	Days Saved Lifetime	Annual Value	Lifetime Value
Dehumidifier drain hose fix	5	21.7	45.1	$1,083	$54,167

The U.S. Army's Seminal Moment: Boots and Blouses (MACRO)

I joined the Army (NYARNG) in 1997 and went to Basic Training and Military Police (MP) School at Fort McClellan, Alabama. A major requirement for MPs was that uniforms be heavily starched (sharp creases) and that boots have a mirror-shine. I understood the reasoning, but I thought it was a major waste of time.

In 2004, the U.S. Army did something radical (by Army standards): it subtracted effort. It replaced ironed, starched uniforms and shined leather boots with non-iron uniforms and no-polish suede. It even changed the regulation to *prohibit* ironing of the new uniforms. In so doing, it eliminated two rituals that had drained soldiers' time for decades. No one called it Strategic Laziness (for if they did, it never would have come to pass), but that's exactly what it was. The replacement wasn't just more comfortable; it was strategically frictionless. Across the entire force, including the Reserves and National Guard, 34.7 million man-hours were reclaimed annually. That translates to more than $1.04 billion in labor value, every year. And that's before you count another $45 million saved in starch, polish, and hardware like irons.

And for the perfectionists who were previously dry cleaning? The actual out-of-pocket amount savings is staggering (over $1,200 a year per soldier). The new uniforms also used Velcro for rank and patches, and pins for skill identifiers, saving even more time and money (you used to have to get that stuff sewn on, at personal expense). This wasn't aesthetics. It was subtraction at strategic scale.

When 700,000 people are repeating the same low-value task, eliminating it isn't cosmetic; it's structural command logic.

This subtraction likely angered a lot of Sergeants Major, but for a cost savings equal to 1.16% of the **total 2004 Army budget** (that's right, all for one uniform change and it reclaimed almost 35,000,000 more training hours to the entire force), even the most strident of traditionalists, the crusty NCOs who love shiny boots and sharp creases, has to take notice, one would think.

But one would be wrong.

It was never studied in depth. Not formally. The U.S. Army's uniform change, one of the most quietly effective systems reforms in modern military history, has been largely ignored in doctrine, organizational analysis, and leadership literature. There's no Field Manual, no Government Accountability Office case study, no post-mortem on what it unlocked. The logistics community didn't herald it. The readiness community didn't benchmark it. And the efficiency community didn't even seem to notice. Perhaps because it wasn't shiny. Perhaps because it killed a sacred ritual. Or perhaps because, in the Army, the subtraction of suffering still doesn't feel like a win (and to be fair, that's often the case).

But it was. It remains a billion-dollar win.

It mortally wounded the shoeshine industry. Kiwi, once synonymous with spit-polished boots, eventually pulled out of the U.S. market in 2024, citing plummeting demand. Dry cleaners near Army posts saw business collapse, with some shops reporting a 50% revenue drop when soldiers stopped starching and pressing five sets of uniforms a week. The impact wasn't isolated. The U.S. Air Force adopted a similar wash-and-wear uniform in 2007, validating the model across branches and creating similar waves in the dry cleaning and shoeshine industries.

The 2004 change wasn't just a uniform update. It was a structural intervention; an elegant kill shot on institutional friction. And we walked right past it.

ROI: Uniform Doctrine Ironing and Shining

Component	Soldiers	Hours Saved (ironing)	Hours Saved (shining)	Total Hours Saved	Time Value Saved	Cost Savings (iron, starch, polish)
Active Duty	494,112	21,411,520	10,705,760	32,117,280	$963,518,400	$32,117,280
Reserves & National Guard	205,879	1,715,658	857,829	2,573,488	$77,204,625	$13,382,135
Total Force	699,991	23,127,178	11,563,589	34,690,768	$1,040,723,025	$45,499,415

ROI: Uniform Doctrine Ironing and Shining Per Soldier

Component	Hours Saved (ironing)	Hours Saved (shining)	Total Hours Saved	Time Value Saved	Cost Savings (iron, starch, polish)	Time Value + Cost Savings
Active Duty	12	4	16	$480	$740	$1,220
Reserves & National Guard	3	1	4	$120	$200	$320

Assumptions Based on 2004 Shining and Ironing Habits
- Active Duty (260 days a year) / Reserve Component (50 days a year)
- 15 minutes shining and ironing per day
- $30/hour average fully loaded soldier rate

ROI: Uniform Doctrine Dry Cleaning

Component	Soldiers	Hours Saved (to and from cleaners)	Hours Saved (waiting)	Total Hours Saved	Time Value Saved	Cost Savings (dry cleaning, pressing, badge sewing)	Time Value + Cost Savings
Active Duty	494,112	5,929,344	1,976,448	7,905,792	$237,173,760	$365,642,880	$602,816,640

Reserves & National Guard	205,879	617,637	205,879	823,516	$24,705,480	$41,175,800	$65,881,280
Total Force	699,991	6,546,981	2,182,327	8,729,308	$261,879,240	$406,818,680	$668,697,920

ROI: Uniform Doctrine Dry Cleaning Per Soldier

Component	Hours Saved (to and from cleaners)	Hours Saved (waiting)	Total Hours Saved	Time Value Saved	Cost Savings (dry cleaning, pressing, badge sewing)	Time Value + Cost Savings
Active Duty	12	4	16	$480	$740	$1,220
Reserves & National Guard	3	1	4	$120	$200	$320

Assumptions Based on 2004 Dry Cleaning Habits
- Active Duty (24 trips a year) / Reserve Component (six trips /year)
- Each trip includes five uniforms at $6 per item
- 30 minutes round-trip
- 10 minutes wait time
- $30/hour average fully loaded soldier rate
- Badge/patch sewing: $20/year

And Now, I Take Off the Uniform

I could write this whole book in fatigues and only focus on the military. The military is a masterclass in enforced routine and a playground for those of us wired to optimize inside the constraints. Shine boots once. Hack the hospital corners. Know what gets inspected and what doesn't. That's Efficient Laziness in its purest form.

But this isn't a military manual. It's a life manual. And while the tactics cross over, most of you aren't standing in formation (anymore). You're running teams, households, businesses. You're juggling kids, deadlines, and inboxes, not rifles and rucks.

So we'll stop here. We'll hang up the uniform and return to the broader mission: building systems that reclaim time, energy, and money—no matter your rank or wardrobe.

Just don't forget the second- and third-order effects. The hidden cost of a high-shine boot. The rework loop of ironing a uniform just to get yelled at, smoked, or sweat through 10 minutes later. That stuff burns time and morale. Reclamations are where we win. In combat. In kitchens. In corner offices. This book is about living like it.

Strategic Laziness: The Diagnostic Test

Before you dive into the chapters, take a minute to audit your current bandwidth fitness. This isn't a personality test. It's a systems diagnostic. Rate each item as 1 (Yes) or 0 (No). Only count it if it's active, repeatable, and saves you time. At the end, total your score and check your status.

#	Subtraction System	Yes (1) / No (0)
SECTION I: Strategic Foundations		
1	I start tasks when they can run without me ("Start Necessary Movement")	
2	I calculate ROI on time before committing to habits or systems	
3	I use planning tools like Troop Leading Procedures (TLPs) to reverse-plan deliverables	
4	I identify and follow desire paths instead of using brute-force effort	
5	I apply the Strategic Architect lens to system design (I'll teach you how!)	
SECTION II: Work Like a Weapon		
6	I use the T/C/S format (Task/Condition/Standard) when assigning tasks	
7	I reduce email load with templates, canned responses, and group my inbox by threads	
8	I batch messages and turn off real-time alerts	
9	I limit meetings to agenda-based or asynchronous formats	
10	I apply the 1/3 Planning –2/3 Execution rule to protect deep work blocks	
11	I use hotkeys to eliminate precise mouse movements and clicks	
12	I delegate using authority, automation, or logic	
13	My team runs independently due to supervision systems (backbriefs)	
14	I align outputs with approval systems	
SECTION III: First Routines		
15	My morning routine omits unnecessary decisions and prep	
16	I wear decision-free clothing and use prepositioned gear	
17	I use slip-on shoes or fast-transition gear	
18	I pre-pack my bag and prep items the night before	
19	I combine hygiene tasks (e.g. shave + shower)	

20	I skip ironing, folding, bed-making, tie-tying, toothpaste top-unscrewing	
21	I use visual systems (externalized, kid-friendly tools that replace verbal reminders with visual cues) for kid routines	
SECTION IV: Home Base		
22	I've automated or delegated recurring chores	
23	I use shared lists and/or repeat orders for groceries	
24	I've optimized appliance ROI (robot vac, dehumidifier, etc.)	
25	I've created elder/childcare plans that reduce daily drag	
26	My family can function without me for at least 24 hours	
27	I keep pre-packed go bags ready for common situations	
SECTION V: Subtract to Learn		
28	I eat a default breakfast and/or lunch to reduce decisions	
29	I batch or modularize dinner prep	
30	I use time-saving cooking tools (e.g. air fryer)	
31	I've solved hydration with a go-to system	
32	I rarely snack reactively due to consistent food routines	
33	I help cognitive load with passive (i.e. audiobooks) and retrieval-based learning (i.e. summarizing from memory)	
34	I skip ads and adjust playback speed to compress learning	
SECTION VI: Work by Design		
35	I walk, run, or bike to work to repurpose commute time	
36	I've eliminated or minimized my commute	
37	I work from home with a structured, repeatable system	
38	I use block scheduling to shape my workday	
39	I design time blocks intentionally (not all time is fungible)	
40	I preserve slack time for family, emergencies, or resets	

Score: _____ / 40

Archetype Scoring

Score Range	Title	Interpretation
0–10	The Grinder	Running on effort, not systems. Start subtracting.
11–20	The Overleveraged	Fragments of structure, but drag still dominates.
21–30	The Architect-in-Training	Gaining leverage, but there's still clutter.

| 31–37 | The High-Leverager | A fine-tuned system, with just a few friction points left. |
| 38+ | Strategic Architect | You've deleted almost every nonessential drag vector. The system runs without you. |

General Kurt von Hammerstein-Equord:

"I divide my officers into four groups. There are clever, diligent, stupid, and lazy officers. Usually two characteristics are combined.

Some are clever and diligent; their place is the General Staff.
The next lot are stupid and lazy; they make up 90 percent of every army and are suited to routine duties.

Anyone who is both clever and lazy is qualified for the highest leadership duties, because he possesses the intellectual clarity and the composure necessary for difficult decisions.

One must beware of anyone who is stupid and diligent; he must not be entrusted with any responsibility because he will always cause only mischief."

Hammerstein-Equord Archetype Matrix		
	Clever	**Stupid**
Diligent	**Grinder:** Planning tacticians. Excellent executors. Excel in environments with structure, oversight, and targets. **Role:** Operational planning, detail execution.	**System Saboteur:** Fast-moving liability. Burns time, trust, and systems through unchecked effort. **Role:** Reassign or remove from decision-making tracks.
Lazy	**Strategic Architect:** High command material. Ruthless in focus, efficient in execution. Delegates what doesn't move the mission. **Role:** Strategic clarity, system design, high leverage.	**Drone:** Non-disruptive baseline. Capable in clear, repetitive systems. No initiative, but no chaos. **Role:** Guardrails required; safe for templated tasks.

Quick Start: Your First 10 Systems

If you're overwhelmed by the full system, start here.

These are the **10 highest-ROI Subtraction Systems** for immediate impact. You can adopt most in less than a day, and they'll return time for years.

1. **Stop making your bed**: Saves one to two minutes per day, six hours a year, instantly.
2. **Default breakfast**: Eliminates daily food decisions and morning friction.
3. **Pre-packed go bag or work bag**: Saves a few minutes daily; prevents forgotten items.
4. **No-decision wardrobe** (set rotation): Reduces cognitive load and speeds morning launch.
5. **Calendar audit** (1/3 Planning–2/3 Execution rule): Restores control over your time landscape.
6. **Hotkeys for common tasks**: Saves dozens of precision micro-clicks per day, thousands per year.
7. **Email templates**: Avoids repeated drafting; boosts throughput immediately.
8. **Start Necessary Movement**: Enabling tasks to run without input is the fastest way to reclaim momentum under load.
9. **Bottled water system**: Ensures hydration with zero decision drag or cost.
10. **Visual systems for kids** (if applicable): Offloads memory and stress for both adults and children.

Start with one per day. Reassess your time and energy gain weekly.

Subtraction Systems don't exist in isolation; they reinforce each other. This is the power of the *System Stack*: batching your inbox creates blocks for deep work; deep work frees bandwidth for high-leverage delegation; delegation enables system autonomy. Like architecture, these systems are designed to interlock. Stack them correctly, and the gains compound. You'll see this logic throughout the book, especially when one Subtraction System creates the conditions for another. This isn't a grab-bag of tips, it's an operating system. Build it accordingly.

SECTION I: *Strategic Foundations*

Think Like a Builder; Move Like a Minimalist

This section equips you with the mental models and planning tools to stop reacting and start architecting your time and energy.

A Subtraction System is anything you build once to save time, thought, or energy repeatedly. If it runs without you re-deciding, re-touching, or re-worrying, it's a Subtraction System. It enables Strategic Laziness.

The Price Tag on Time

I used to iron my shirts in the morning. It wasn't hard. It wasn't long. It was just part of the routine.

Then one day, running late for a meeting, I stared at the clock while plugging in the iron and did the math. Not metaphorical math. Real ROI.

How much time had I burned smoothing out collars? How many reps had I done of fill-the-reservoir, wait-for-the-light, flatten-the-sleeve? At three minutes per shirt, five shirts a week, 50 weeks a year, for 10 years, that's 125 hours. More than five full days.

And what did I get for it? Slightly crisper cuffs and an ironed shirt that I immediately covered with a suit jacket.

That day, I bought wrinkle-resistant shirts. Not the cheap ones; I sprung for Charles Tyrwhitt's non-iron dress shirts, the type you pull out of the dryer and hang up. Great hand, relatively crisp (crisp enough, anyway). And I never unwillingly touched an iron again. I didn't "buy convenience." I eliminated friction.

Time is money. But more than that, it's momentum. Subtraction Systems aren't hacks. They're decisions you make once that pay you forever. If you're not asking, "What's the cost of this thing I do every day?" you're still playing checkers.

Chapter 1: What Strategic Laziness Is (and Isn't)

Strategic Laziness isn't a joke. It isn't an excuse to cut corners or work less. It's the discipline of knowing which corners must be cut because they shouldn't exist in the first place.

It's not about doing nothing. It's about doing less of the wrong things so you can do more of the right ones, with less friction, fewer decisions, and more control.

Strategic Laziness is not sloth. It is subtraction with intent.

If you're reading this, you've probably already been grinding. You've probably been told to hustle harder, wake up earlier, and build the plane while flying it. And maybe you've started to suspect that's not a plan, it is burnout dressed up as work ethic.

This book is the antidote.

Strategic Laziness is a conscious decision to reclaim your time by redesigning the systems you live inside. Not with theory. With practice. It's about removing friction, stacking actions, and reclaiming the compound interest of attention and output.

It means being ruthless about effort-to-outcome ratio. It means finding the system that gives you back 1,000 hours a year, not by working more, but by plugging the slow leaks you didn't know were bleeding you dry.

You don't have to optimize every second. You don't have to act like a robot. But you do have to stop wasting your best hours on inboxes, meetings, errands, laundry loops, and treadmill routines that yield nothing but fatigue.

Strategic Laziness is:
- Drinking water from a YETI instead of buying 100 plastic bottles
- Wearing a non-iron shirt that saves 10 hours a year in prep
- Using audio learning while commuting so your brain doesn't idle
- Canceling standing meetings that produce zero change
- Saying "no" to status games that yield no strategic outcome
  - Status games: performative behaviors that exist only to signal prestige, hierarchy, or conformity
- Stacking a 30-minute run with a 30-minute commute and reclaiming both

It's not about shortcuts. It's about building systems that don't need you to push them once they're in motion. If you have to keep touching it, it's not a system; it's a leash.

This book will not make you rich in 90 days. It won't give you abs (sorry, I know, but you'll have more time to build them, if you choose). It won't teach you how to manifest.

What it will do is show you how to reclaim time you've already earned, remove drag from your systems, and build bandwidth into a life that doesn't break down when you step away.

That's not laziness. That's leadership. That's the Subtraction System. That's what I built here.

A 2021 study in *Nature* found that humans systematically fail to consider subtraction to improve systems. We add features, rules, tasks. But subtraction is often the most elegant, and ignored, solution.[2]

Archetype: The Strategic Architect (Success Case)

Summary: A mission-driven professional who builds systems to protect time, energy, and clarity. They don't hustle. They construct. They embed. They outmaneuver. They're not loud, but they're lethal—in meetings, in bandwidth, in execution.

They're not defined by one domain. They're **cross-domain** capable:
- Leadership like a U.S. Army Infantry Officer
- Diplomacy like a U.S. Foreign Service Officer
- Systems like a DoD International Project Manager
- Bandwidth like a parent with 90 minutes and a mission

This book isn't just for professionals. It's for people building a life system. Strategic Laziness is the doctrine. Becoming a Strategic Architect is the goal.

Traits of the Strategic Architect:
- Intent-First: Doesn't need all the answers, just the direction and constraints.
- Bandwidth-Stacker: Builds systems that create more time than they consume.
- Delegation-Fluent: Doesn't hoard work; designs systems to carry weight.
- Quietly Dangerous: Understates capabilities. Overdelivers.
- Clarity Addict: Kills ambiguity early. Reduces drag across all domains.
- Tactically Empathetic: Reads rooms, teams, and timing. Calibrates output to the situation.

Book Structure as Strategic Architect Thinking

You're not just subtracting tasks. You're **building a system**, a personal command architecture. Each one trains a capability. Not just a time-saver, but a force multiplier. Each section of this book trains a core function of the Strategic Architect role:

---

[2] Gabrielle S. Adams, Benjamin A. Converse, Andrew H. Hales, and Leidy E. Klotz, "People Systematically Overlook Subtractive Changes," *Nature* 592 (2021): 258–261.

Real-World Focus	System You Build
Morning Prep	Fast-Start Routine
Wardrobe & Grooming	No-Decision Dressing
Packing	Grab-and-Go Prep
Meetings	Decision-Making System
Email & Notifications	Inbox Control System
Calendars	Time Mapping
Chores & Errands	Home Task Automation
Parenting Systems	Family Routine Design
Financial + Home Ops	Household Systems
Food & Hydration	Easy Nutrition
Learning Systems	Smart Input Habits
Work From Home	Focus Environment
Supervision	Clarity-Based Leadership

Archetype: The Grinder (Failure Case)

The Grinder works hard. That's *the* problem.

He wakes at 6:15 a.m. Alarm off. Notifications on. Slack notifications already waiting, one from his boss, one from his kid's school. No plan for either.

Mental load: +10 min/day just to reorient.

He's already behind, but he stops to **make the bed anyway.** Because some Four-Star Admiral once said to.

(2 min lost, 0 min gained)

He gets dressed:
- Ties his tie. **(1 min)**
- Shirt needs ironing. Too late. Digs out a backup that's wrinkled **(2 more min)** (still looks disheveled)

(3 min lost)

Coffee wasn't prepped.
- Fumbles filters.
- Spills grounds.
- Forgets to refill the reservoir.
- Microwaves his mug twice.

(5 min lost, + cortisol)

Then dumps in two large scoops of sugar.
+200 calories/day = +15 lbs./year

He leaves late. Waze normally says 37 minutes. But leaving late, it's 47 minutes of stop-and-go. No podcast. No audiobook. Just brake lights and self-recrimination. **Zero learning. Zero decompression.**

He walks into work flustered.

Inbox: 40+ emails. No filters. No batch windows. No templates. Spends the first hour clicking, skimming, retyping things he's sent before.

Email drift: +1 hr./day

Then come the meetings.
- Three before lunch.
- One didn't have an agenda.
- Two could've been Slack messages.

Total waste: 3 hours

Lunch: the saddest of desk sandwiches.

Workout: "Tomorrow."

Dinner: drive-through.

Kid's soccer game: missed again.

He's tired. Up 15 pounds. Calendar full. Inbox full. Mind full. Still believes if he just works harder, things will click.

But they won't. Because effort without architecture is drag.

Daily Cost of a Life Without Subtraction Systems

Leak	Time Lost (min)	Dollar Equivalent (@$50/hr)
Morning Mental Drift	10	$8
Performative Discipline (bed)	2	$2
Wardrobe Friction	3	$3
Coffee Chaos	5	$4
Commute (no learning)	47	$39
Email Drift	60	$50
Meetings Without ROI	90	$75
Sugar Health Cost		Major future health burden
Total	**217**	**$181**

The Grinder is down 3½ hours and $181 before lunch. Every day. Here's the annual damage:

Annual Cost of a Life Without Subtraction Systems

Metric	Value
Workdays Burned	~48/year
Time Lost Annually	~950 hours
Financial Opportunity Cost	$43,400+
Health Drift	+15 lbs./year
Relationship Strain	Rising
Professional Momentum	Flatlined

This guy isn't underperforming because he's lazy. He's losing because he thinks effort is more important than a system. And that's the most expensive lie he's ever believed.

How do you escape this system? How do you find more time? How do you save more money?

The answer is: you already have the time and the money in lost bandwidth. And you need to reclaim them.

Chapter 2: The Discipline of Subtraction

Subtraction seems harder than addition. In school, in business, in life, anything (or anyone) can pile on. More meetings, more emails, more apps, more habits. But real discipline is knowing what to cut, when to cut it, and having the judgment to know it won't come back to bite you.

That's the core of **Strategic Laziness**: discipline by subtraction. It's not minimalism. Minimalism is aesthetic. Whereas subtraction is operational. You're not aiming for clean lines on a whiteboard. You're aiming for less drag on your actual life. This book is full of tactics, but they all share one operating principle: if something doesn't deliver more than it costs, **cut it loose and don't give it a second, costly thought.** If a task offers no strategic gain, delete it. If a system has a manual loop that can be automated or avoided, substitute it or stack it.

Subtraction is how you reclaim time, attention, and energy. Not by doing more *gestures expansively* **stuff**, but by doing **fewer** things, better.

You subtract to recover:
- Time you gave away to friction
- Money you leaked through habits
- Energy you burned on rituals with no return
- Mental capacity spent holding things your system should be handling

This book doesn't ask you to become a productivity freak. It asks you to think like a Strategic Architect: assess your life like a system, and build with one goal: maximum return on minimal input.

You're not failing because you're under-disciplined; you're failing because you're outnumbered. Subtraction is how you change the odds.

Discipline by subtraction offers structure, not stress. It enables fewer moving parts and more forward motion.

Here's the rule: **Every time you subtract the right thing, what's left becomes more powerful.** Now let's start cutting.

Chapter 3: How to Calculate ROI on Time

This book is built on a single idea: your time has value. Measurable, dollar-based value. That means we can calculate ROI for almost every habit, tool, or system in your life.

It's not about being cold or clinical; it's about being clear.

Step One: Assign a Dollar Value to Your Time

We use $50/hour as a conservative benchmark. You can adjust that up or down, but the math holds: if you save 30 minutes a day, five days a week, you're recapturing 130 hours per year. At $50/hour, that's $6,500 annually.

If that sounds like a stretch, consider this: You'd pay a plumber $150 an hour to fix your pipes. You'd pay a lawyer $500 an hour to draft a contract. Your time is more expensive than both, because it's finite.

This isn't aspirational; it's practical. You are already spending your time like money. We're just putting it on a balance sheet.

Step Two: Identify Time Savings

Time ROI shows up in three forms:

> **Eliminated Tasks** – You just don't do it anymore.
> (e.g. no ironing, no bed-making, no dry-cleaning runs)

> **Stacked Tasks** – You do multiple things at once.
> (e.g. biking to work + completing your workout + listening to a podcast)

> **Accelerated Tasks** – You do it faster, with less friction.
> (e.g. pre-packed gear, email templates, home systems)

Each chapter in this book demonstrates how to reclaim time in one of those three ways.

Step Three: Multiply It Out

Calculating the Total Value of a Time-Saving System

Factor	Formula	Example
Daily savings	Minutes saved × 260 (workdays) or 365 (daily)	5 min/day × 260 = 1,300 min/year
Annual time saved	Minutes ÷ 60 = hours	1,300 min = 21.7 hours/year
Annual cash value	Hours × $50	21.7 × $50 = $1,085
Lifetime value	Annual hours × 50 years	21.7 × 50 = 1,085 hours = $54,250

You can use this math on anything:
- The one minute you save by not tying a tie = $260/year
- Swapping dry-cleaning for machine-wash shirts = $910/year
- Canceling one (just one?) unnecessary meeting a week = $2,600/year

It adds up fast. You're not saving pennies. You're compounding efficiency.

Every dollar you don't spend is a system that reroutes value. When used strategically, even small financial subtractions, done consistently, can be worth thousands. Here's how.

Sidebar: Kill the Latte, Kill the Debt

Say you spend $5 every weekday at Starbucks. You don't have to kill it; just cut it in half. Instead of $25 a week, spend $12.50. Apply the other $12.50 toward a credit card balance.

Scenario:
- $5,000 credit card debt
- 18% APR
- Minimum payment: $125/month
- Additional $50/month via your new "latte subtraction system"

Result:
- Time to repay debt without the extra $50: **~58 months**
- Time to repay with the $50/week subtraction: **~35 months**
- Interest saved: **~$1,600+**
- Bandwidth gained: **~2 years without monthly payments**

The system isn't just about the coffee. It's about eliminating passive leakage, then reclaiming agency. Even small subtractions become massive multipliers when they compound across interest, fees, stress, and time. In this case, a single Subtraction System buys back months of freedom.

The Real ROI

Money is one metric. But it's not the whole picture. Time ROI buys you:
- Sanity
- Focus
- Presence with your family
- Freedom from decision fatigue
- Energy for your actual mission

- Time for luxuries

ROI isn't just dollars; it's **bandwidth**. If you had an extra hour today, what would you spend it on? This book is your system to find that hour. Over and over again.

Some systems may overlap. ROI values are illustrative and assume independent execution.

Chapter 4: Mission Planning for Real Life (TLPs)

In the U.S. Army, the Troop Leading Procedures (TLPs) are how you move from chaos to ordered execution. This sequence takes a vague, sometimes bad plan and turns it into something your team can pull off. Over time, I realized: this wasn't just doctrine, it was a bandwidth-reclamation framework. TLP #4, *Start Necessary Movement* (SNM), is my favorite and the one most applicable to creating systems. SNM legitimizes imperfect action with incomplete information.

Most planning systems try to optimize clarity. The TLPs optimize *action*, and you provide the clarity filter for the action. Each TLP is a discrete step designed to buy you back time, reduce friction, and prevent failure. That's bandwidth.

I use them constantly, in leadership, in parenting, in diplomacy, and in business. Here's how each TLP reclaims a different form of bandwidth.

1. Receive the Mission

Bandwidth Type Reclaimed: Cognitive

Many leaders burn energy chasing details that don't matter. The first thing the TLPs teach you is how to extract signal (useful info) from noise.

An Army OPORD (Operations Order) is dense and often written for higher levels than you need (e.g. it's written for a battalion of 600 soldiers and you're a platoon leader of 45 soldiers). It's easy to get lost in it, unless you learn to filter and extract. When receiving an oral OPORD, junior officers (and especially Cadets) make the mistake of trying to write down everything. I watched many try to keep up, scribbling furiously while missing the intent entirely. I did this at first, too. But later, I learned to extract only the necessary and valuable information. After that, I never wrote everything down. I focused on the *commander's intent*, the *mission*, and the *non-negotiables*. Everything else was noise.

Business Translation: Stop writing down everything in meetings. Extract what matters: the what, the why, and what *can't* be dropped.

Bandwidth Gained: You spend less time rechecking, reinterpreting, and re-explaining. You operate with clarity, not chaos.
- Usefulness: 10/10

- Time Share: 10%

2. Issue the Warning Order

Bandwidth Type Reclaimed: Time

You don't need a perfect plan to start moving. Good leaders build bandwidth by getting others ready before the full picture is clear. Bad leaders hoard information until it's too late to use. When others know that a task is incoming shortly, they can run their own TLPs, independent of you.

Business Translation: Send a pre-kickoff email. Tell people to stand by, not stand still. "Team, project incoming. Expect calendar drops. Early prep = future win."

Bandwidth Gained: You reduce latency. While you finalize the plan, others are already warming up.
- Usefulness: 7/10
- Time Share: 5%

3. Make a Tentative Plan

Bandwidth Type Reclaimed: Planning Latency

Perfect plans are slow. Rough plans that invite feedback move faster. This step isn't about solving every problem; it's about putting a scaffolding in place.

Business Translation: Use a slide deck, whiteboard, or document to sketch a 70% solution. Build it to break and improve.

Bandwidth Gained: You reduce time spent reinventing. You prevent bottlenecks. And you include others early enough to matter.
- Usefulness: 9/10
- Time Share: 15%

4. Start Necessary Movement (My favorite!)

Bandwidth Type Reclaimed: Execution Time

This is where many people fail, military or civilian. They wait for the plan to be perfect before starting anything. That's a waste. SNM is about launching tasks that can proceed without delay.

Military Examples:
- Move units to staging areas
- Start vehicle checks
- Begin your own prep

- Check/pack gear

Business Translations:
- Book refundable venues
- Post job openings before the org chart is finalized
- Send onboarding docs
- Notify partner teams
- Keep track of your annual accomplishments as they are completed

Strategic Architect Rule
If you have to babysit it, it's not SNM; it's a leash. In other words: If it only works when you're watching, it's not a system.

Bandwidth Gained: You get a head start on every parallel task. You stop serializing execution and start layering time.
- Usefulness: 10/10
- Time Share: 20%

5. Recon the Objective

Bandwidth Type Reclaimed: Risk Buffer

You can't always see the objective. But you can always learn something. Recon isn't about luxury; it's about risk management.

In Iraq, I often had to plan raids with no physical recons or satellite imagery. Our intel shop required three days to provide imagery (very problematic for kinetic units). I needed three minutes. I used Google Earth, printed out imagery of the objective, and did the recon with key leaders. Was it perfect? No. Was it better than flying blind? Definitely.

Business Translations: Site visits, demos, mock-ups, early user tests, focus groups. Whatever gives you just enough to move forward.

Bandwidth Gained: Fewer surprises and fewer emergency pivots; cleaner execution.
- Usefulness: 8/10
- Time Share: 10%

6. Complete the Plan

Bandwidth Type Reclaimed: System Stability

By the time you finalize the plan, wheels are already turning. That's the power of SNM. Now you're not starting cold; you're locking in timelines, syncing teams, and closing gaps. SNM meshes nicely with Newton's First Law of Motion: objects in motion tend to stay in motion unless acted upon by an outside force (friction, anyone?). Momentum is a real thing, both in practical terms and psychologically.

Business Translations: Final check-ins with stakeholders. Briefs updated. Tools ready. Redundancies in place.

Bandwidth Gained: You remove execution friction and reduce future oversight requirements.
- Usefulness: 9/10
- Time Share: 15%

7. Issue the Order

Bandwidth Type Reclaimed: Alignment

Issuing the order isn't about telling people what to do; it's about confirming they really understand. That's what a *backbrief*, a quick verbal confirmation of comprehension, does.

Ask:
- What's your role?
- What's the deadline?
- What's your contingency plan (Plan C? Plan D?)?

Business Translation: Five minutes of clarity up front prevents hours of cleanup later.

Bandwidth Gained: You don't have to redo anything. You don't chase missed expectations.
- Usefulness: 10/10
- Time Share: 10%

8. Supervise

Bandwidth Type Reclaimed: Cognitive Load

When you've effectively executed the first seven steps, supervision becomes observation. You're not fighting fires. You're watching systems work.

Business Translations: Monitor dashboards, not people. Check sync points, not every detail.

Bandwidth Gained: You get to think again. You free your brain for actual leadership.
- Usefulness: 8/10
- Time Share: 15%

Strategic Architect Rule
If you're doing everything, you're planning incorrectly. Each TLP is a tool for buying back time, attention, or momentum. Use them well and you don't just manage your team; you multiply it.

Chapter 5: Desire Paths and System Design

Desire paths are the worn dirt trails that cross through lawns, behind benches, or cut corners, beaten into existence by repeated human decisions to leave the sidewalk for a faster way. They don't follow the official blueprint. They follow reality.

Subtraction Systems follow a similar logic as a desire path and you need to get on that path.

A landscape architect decides where the sidewalk goes. But a person walks where it actually makes sense, and that's the path that wins. Following a sidewalk just to follow a sidewalk adds friction.

Strategic Laziness Is a Desire Path

Every Subtraction System in this book is a desire path.

It's the frictionless route cut through outdated habits, needless rituals, and performative struggle. It doesn't rebel against structure; it questions it. And where the map wastes your time, it redraws the map. Strategic Laziness isn't about defiance. It's about judgment.

Efficiency isn't rebellion. It's judgment. The best path is forged by walking smarter than the map.

You don't guard your bandwidth by doing more. You protect it by doing less, better.

Walk the Path Until It Becomes the Real One

You won't find the systems in this book in your HR onboarding packet. They're not standard operating procedures. But they work, because they're built from lived constraints, not legacy rules.
- You pre-pack your gym bag not because the Drill Sergeant said so, but because it prevents skipped workouts.
- You use pre-written email templates not to be formulaic, but to protect your mental focus.
- You run to work not to make a statement, but to merge two tasks that would otherwise cost you two hours each into a singular, one-hour task.

Every one of those is a desire path. You walked it once. Then again. Now it's permanent.

How to Spot Desire Paths in Your Own Life

You don't need a city planner to find them. Just pay attention to where you already cut corners, intentionally or not.

Ask yourself:
- Where do I always deviate from the "official" process?
- What steps do I skip, but get the same result?
- What routines do I dread, stall, or rush through?
- What friction do I constantly work around?

Those aren't accidents. They're system design notes from your subconscious. Codify them. Refine them. Build your blueprint around what already works.

Make the Efficient Path the Default One

You don't fight the pattern. You formalize it. Strategic Laziness does the same thing. We detect what works, strip away what doesn't, and lock in the wins. You can't eliminate all friction. But you can refuse to suffer the same pointless drag twice. The first time you find a shortcut, it's intuition. The second time, it's a habit. The third time, it should be a system. Walk it enough times, and the dirt path becomes the real one.

Chapter 6: The Power of Starting Necessary Movement

Humans often want to wait for clarity before acting. Leaders usually don't have that luxury. In every domain—household, business, military, diplomacy—waiting to act until you have every answer is how you get outpaced, outflanked, or outright embarrassed.

Starting Necessary Movement is the countermeasure. It's the discipline of launching the pieces that can move, **even if the rest of the plan is still foggy**. You're not being reckless. You're building parallel pathways so that when the final order hits, you're already halfway there.

The biggest time gains in my life haven't come from working faster. They've come from moving earlier. From starting 10 things at once, knowing half of them would auto-run while I focused on the rest. SNM isn't efficiency theater; it's real leverage.

The three case studies that follow, household, business, and military, aren't theory. They're blueprints for how to reclaim hours and reduce drag under pressure. The common thread? Every one of them shows what happens when you *start before you're 100% ready*.

Tales From the Field – If It Can Move Now, Move It Now

The rule is always the same: if something can move now, move it. In combat, that meant starting the mission without waiting for the perfect piece of intel. In diplomacy, it meant sending the brief to those who needed to see it, not waiting for everyone to clear it. SNM isn't about recklessness. It's about preserving momentum in a world designed to stall you.

13. Household Case Study: International Move with Kids

Scenario: You're moving your family from New York to Trinidad and Tobago in 45 days for a new assignment. Your spouse is working full-time, and your kid is in elementary school.

Mission: Complete an international move and reduce stress, lost items, or child meltdowns.

Critical SNM Tasks: All of these can start before your final housing or school situation is nailed down.

Task	SNM Action	How It Pays Off

	Email three top schools asking for process & deadlines	Reduces school scramble later
School Search	Email three top schools asking for process & deadlines	Reduces school scramble later
Passport & Docs	Book passport renewals; gather birth certificates	Avoids government delays
Movers	Request three quotes + dates for international movers	Locks availability
Kids' Transition	Order books about Trinidad and Tobago; teach five local facts	Lowers emotional friction
Financial	Notify banks of international travel	Prevents fraud blocks
Housing	Create housing criteria doc + spreadsheet	Streamlines final search
Health	Schedule appointments now	Avoids last-minute insurance gap
Utilities	Create a list of must-cancel + set reminders	Removes final week mental clutter

Bandwidth Created: By week 2, half the logistical load is moving forward without daily input, freeing you to focus on higher-value problems like job onboarding and childcare.

14. Business Case Study: Jammock Launch with Zero Staff

Scenario: You're just some guy with a full-time job and no business experience, but you've built a prototype hammock that fits on a Jeep's roll bars. You have no staff, no capital, and no formal plan, just a product idea and a bit of free time.

Mission: Test the market, create a legitimate product, and launch online with zero downtime from your full-time job.

Critical SNM Tasks

Task	SNM Action	How It Paid Off
Product Naming	Bought the domain Jammock.com immediately after idea hit	Locked in brand identity before legal or production started
Legal Structure	Filed LLC paperwork online before any sales occurred	Enabled early revenue collection and liability protection
Prototype Testing	Used personal Jeep to test prototypes in real-world use	Received immediate feedback on design before scaling up

Manufacturing	Found and contacted multiple U.S.-based canvas suppliers	Built sourcing pipeline while branding and sales were still conceptual
Website	Built a basic landing page using WordPress + PayPal	Captured preorders before the full product line was ready
IP Protection	Filed provisional patent and trademark paperwork	Protected future value with minimal upfront cost
Marketing	Created and mailed discount magnets to place on parked Jeeps	Passive, zero-cost marketing that ran in the background
Distribution	Used USPS flat-rate boxes and online click-n-ship tools	Avoided warehousing delays and streamlined solo fulfillment

Bandwidth Created: SNM allowed branding, manufacturing, legal, and marketing efforts to run in parallel, without full-time effort. By the time demand spiked, infrastructure was already in motion. Jammock sold 15,000+ units and generated $1.3M in revenue with minimal input cost and no outside investors.

15. Military Case Study: Platoon Raid Planning

Scenario: You receive an order at 2300 for a 0300 raid on a suspected High-Value Target (HVT) living in a compound, but your platoon just came off an 18-hour mission and you are scrambling.

Mission: Clear and secure the compound with minimal civilian disruption and zero friendly casualties. Detain or kill the HVT. Impound all electronic devices.

Critical SNM Tasks

Task	SNM Action	How It Pays Off
Weapons Check	Order squad leaders to perform Preventative Maintenance Checks & Services immediately	Ensures no last-minute equipment failures
Comms Prep	Have Radio Telephone Operators verify radios, batteries, encryption keys	Prevents mission issues due to dead communications
Movement Plan	Coordinate truck and route logistics while target is being confirmed	Locks convoy readiness
Intelligence	Request updated Intelligence, Surveillance, & Reconnaissance from the	Provides latest info on enemy movements and behaviors

	intelligence officer, even without grid confirmation	
Medical Prep	Set casualty evacuation point(s)	Enables care under fire without pause
ROE Brief	Update soldiers on the Rules of Engagement	Smooths decision-making under pressure

Bandwidth Created

By 0100 hours, the platoon is 60% ready without knowing the final grid coordinates. When the full OPORD drops at 0200, you're adjusting dials, not spinning up engines.

Strategic Architect Rule

If a task doesn't depend on the final plan, start it now. You're not delegating blindly. You're reclaiming time from the front edge of chaos.

Chapter 7: Logic Compression – Subtracting What Doesn't Matter

Core Problem

People don't have a time problem. They have a *logic problem*.

They waste bandwidth chasing untested assumptions, solving the wrong problems, or defending ideas they've never even audited. They respond instead of reasoning. They optimize surface tasks while ignoring the flawed logic underneath. Then they wonder why the friction never stops.

- A political candidate spends hours crafting the perfect Instagram post that persuades exactly zero voters (and actually alienates a non-zero amount).

16. A rifle platoon leader delays clearing a rooftop because no one had codified what to do when intel is vague, so his platoon takes contact while waiting for clarity that never comes.
17. A U.S. Ambassador burns an hour clearing talking points for an issue the Mission had already resolved, because no one built a system to suppress resolved problems from resurfacing.

Every bad decision you skip is bandwidth you never lose. Every thought loop you close is one less cycle draining your attention. This isn't about working faster—it's about not working on the wrong thing.

This chapter is the system behind the systems. Because without clean logic, every habit you form risks becoming a beautifully polished, completely useless mistake.

The Cost of Confused Thinking

Confused effort looks exactly like dedicated work—until you audit the outcome. Then, oops.

A bad idea isn't just inefficient. It's *expensive*. It multiplies its own cost. Every minute spent acting on bad logic is another minute locked into a losing bet. You email the wrong stakeholder. You build the wrong deck. You optimize a task that didn't need to exist. And then you double down, because sunk costs feel safer than starting over.

There's a reason "Sunk Cost" gets its own fallacy.

Logic Compression: the deliberate practice of distilling complex, multi-variable decision structures into simple, reusable rules that eliminate ambiguity, reduce recursion, and accelerate high-fidelity action. It substitutes ad hoc reasoning with codified logic, allowing decisions to be made once and executed many times. At its core, logic compression is the architecture of clarity: it subtracts unnecessary thought loops by replacing them with pre-vetted if/then systems that preserve intent while minimizing cognitive drag.

Failure Case: Amateur Logic and the Butcher's Cleaver

Bad logic compression isn't neutral—it's actively dangerous.

Picture this: a new "efficiency task force" is set loose on a bureaucracy. Their orders? Cut anything that seems redundant, bloated, or old. But no one on the team understands the logic of the systems they're dismantling. They've never run a mission, staffed a crisis, or held the line on a budget with real-world consequences. They are not forensic accountants, auditors, or expert consultants.

So, they start slashing. Offices disappear; heck, entire divisons are axed over the weekend. Teams get gutted. Programs with obscure but critical functions get wiped out with the same glee as those running out-of-date websites.

From the outside and to the general public, it looks decisive. From the inside, it's pure chaos. Because they weren't compressing logic—they were butchers hacking at it with meat cleavers instead of a Board Certified, Harvard MD using her scalpel.

This is the cognitive equivalent of a first-year med student walking into surgery and just… cutting. Sure, you can remove an organ. But did you stop to ask whether it regulates blood pressure? Produces hormones? Manages immunity? Did you tie off the blood vessels that fed it? Or did you just think: "Well, it's lumpy and expensive, so out it goes"?

True logic compression subtracts waste by preserving what's functional and eliminating what isn't. Bad compression just subtracts. Blindly. You don't save the system by turning off its warning lights. You save it by wiring them to the right triggers.

Why Logic Saves You Time

You've been told logical systems slow you down. Wrong. They let you *stop solving the same problem five times*. They let you pre-clear choices so you don't have to second-guess them later. They compress your mental stack, reduce emotional overhead, and frontload clarity. Clear logic is the ultimate time-saver: it stops the bullshit before it starts.

What Is Logic Compression?

Logic compression is the practice of distilling complex, branching decision structures into clean, executable rules. It is how professionals scale judgment without scaling chaos. It's the system you use to subtract ambiguity, friction, and delay *before* they hit your calendar.

- In computer science, this is called *reduction*.
- In strategy, it's *doctrine*.
- In this book, it's subtraction at the source.

Where most people waste hours chasing implications, logic compression lets you frontload the thinking once, codify the structure, and move on. It is the *opposite* of reactive. It's how you delete entire classes of bad decisions before they happen.

Logic Compression = Recursion Reduction

This chapter teaches you how to do one thing: collapse infinite forks into finite signals.

Because every time you compress a logic tree into a symbolic rule, you've done something profound:

- You've reduced the number of recursive loops your brain must track.
- You've deleted the need to re-decide the same issue in the future.
- You've subtracted—not just the task, but the *cognitive weight* of the task.

That's not just time saved. It's momentum preserved.

How Logic "Compression" Works in Practice

Author's Note: you might already know or suspect this. This may be new for you, or it may be familiar but just framed differently. Either way, this Logic Compression is one of the most overall important systems in this book.

Step 1: Symbolic Logic – Setup

Let's say we have the following logical statement: If P and (P implies Q), then Q

This statement looks like this in symbolic logic: $(P \land (P \rightarrow Q)) \rightarrow Q$

This is a classic form of Modus Ponens, one of the foundational inference rules in deductive logic.

Step 2: Reduction (Logical Inference)

Here's how it works:

P (Assume P is true)

$P \rightarrow Q$ (If P, then Q)

Therefore: Q

This entire logical stack simplifies into: $P, P \rightarrow Q \Rightarrow Q$

We compressed the reasoning: instead of holding all three statements in your head, we reduce it to a direct path from P and $P \rightarrow Q$ to Q.

So it's not $(P \land (P \rightarrow Q)) \rightarrow Q$. It's just Q.

Step 3: Practical Application of the Above Logical Shorthand (Compression)

Let's translate that into a practical, bandwidth-saving example:

P = "I've automated my bills."

Q = "I don't need to track due dates manually."

So:
- If P is true (you've set up automation),
- And you know $P \rightarrow Q$ (automation eliminates the need to track),
- Then logically, Q follows: you can stop checking your due dates manually.

Instead of thinking about it every month, you collapse the logic tree into a permanent conclusion: "I don't check my bills. It's built in."

Instead of saying "What should I do?" five times a week, you build a logic gate once and just follow the outcome.

That's cognitive compression that ends up compounding. You set up automatic billing, once, and it compounds.

Level One: Campaign Trail Compression (Mundane but Ubiquitous)

The Frame: You're advising a local candidate for office. He's spending two hours a day posting selfies, chasing meaningless endorsements, and responding to trolls. The campaign staff feels busy but disorganized. Everyone's confusing movement with momentum. The candidate sees the campaign as a personal brand project—when in reality, it's just a math problem in disguise.

The Compression Mandate

Every action must be filtered through two recursive questions:
1. Does this action gain us votes?
2. Do the gained votes justify the time and resources spent (ROI, anyone)?
If either answer is "No," the action is killed. Full stop. No sentiment, no inertia, no sunk cost fallacies.

Uncompressed Logic Tree
- V: This task might raise visibility

- W: Visibility might gain a few votes
- X: Endorsements might influence undecideds
- Y: Posting often keeps the base happy
- Z: This feels productive

Resulting logic:

$(V \lor W \lor X \lor Y) \land Z \rightarrow$ Do it again tomorrow

This logic tree rewards *momentum theater,* not outcome. It justifies mediocrity by activity volume.

Compression Logic

Replace the above with one governing rule:

If (Action $\rightarrow$ Votes) and (Votes $\geq$ Cost), then Approve A. Else, Reject A.

Symbolically:
- $(A \rightarrow V), V \geq C \Rightarrow$ Approve A
- $\neg(A \rightarrow V) \lor V < C \Rightarrow$ Reject A

Example, Compressed

- Endorsement from fringe pastor:
  - Gain: +2 votes
  - Loss: –1 vote
  - Time: 4 hours
  - Net vote delta per hour: +0.25

  $\Rightarrow$ Fails cost-benefit test $\rightarrow$ Killed

Campaign Doctrine

This compression transforms political vanity into executable doctrine. It allows small campaigns to compete with larger ones by killing wasted motion. It also cleans the candidate's mental slate for real decisions: field deployment, donor prioritization, and opponent strategy.

What This Unlocks:
- **Time efficiency:** Your day becomes a vote-maximizing engine, not a performance treadmill.
- **Crisis clarity:** Every new opportunity routes through an existing logic filter, not a staff argument.
- **Message discipline:** If it doesn't move votes, it doesn't move your mouth.
- **Mental bandwidth:** Fewer low-return decisions = cleaner mind for big plays.
You're not running for Most Visible. You're running to win.

Level Two: Combat Mission Filter (Moderately Complex)

The Frame: You are a Rifle Platoon Leader in Baghdad, Iraq. The environment is urban, unstable, and wired with ambiguity. Second Squad reports movement on a rooftop across the alley—uncertain identity, unknown intent. Civilians? Spotters? Forward observers? You have seconds to decide.

In infantry doctrine, ambiguity at the tactical level is systematically collapsed using a structure known as Battle Drills, a set of standardized responses to specific battlefield stimuli. These drills represent logic compression in its purest form.

You don't weigh variables. You trigger responses.

Inputs (Conditions C):
- C_1: Movement observed by multiple team members
- C_2: Movement sustained for more than 10 seconds
- C_3: Observers are silhouetted or partially concealed
- C_4: Known insurgent activity in the zone
- C_5: Positive hostile action (e.g., aimed weapon, callout over radio)
- C_6: Presence of civilians in line of fire

Outputs (Actions A):
- A_1: Initiate "Platoon Attack" Battle Drill
- A_2: Shift fire sectors and call for PID (positive identification)
- A_3: Call higher for ISR (intelligence, surveillance, reconnaissance) support
- A_4: Initiate escalation-of-force protocol
- A_5: Mark and bypass; continue mission

Compressed Tactical Logic:
- $C_1 \wedge C_2 \wedge C_3 \wedge C_4 \rightarrow A_1$
- $C_1 \wedge \neg C_5 \wedge C_6 \rightarrow A_2 \wedge A_4$
- $C_1 \wedge \neg C_4 \rightarrow A_3$
- $\neg C_1 \rightarrow A_5$

Each of these logical statements compresses dozens of variables—angle of fire, political risk, urban density, probability of ambush—into instinctive, executable doctrine. No one on the team has to think, "What's the risk calculus of returning fire across rooftops with uncertain identities?" The logic tree is pre-burned into training.

This is what enables action under fire: compressed decision logic deployed in real time.

What This Unlocks:

- **Speed reducing errors:** Soldiers don't think—they act, because thinking was already done in doctrine.
- **Shared cognition:** Every fire team in the platoon follows the same logic structure. No room for variance.
- **Chain-resilient logic:** If a squad leader is hit, the next in line knows exactly what to do.

- **Command clarity:** You aren't micromanaging; you're enforcing compressed logic that everyone already internalized.

Lesson: When lives are on the line, ambiguity must be annihilated—not through brute force, but through structural clarity. The battlefield doesn't wait. Logic must already be compressed and deployed.

Now, let's do it at full speed.

Level Three: Logic at the Edge of Ambiguity (Profoundly Complex)

Compression = Recursion Reduction

At its core, logic compression isn't just about faster decisions—it's about reducing the number of recursive forks a mind must track. Every time we compress ambiguity into structure, we reclaim executive function from the infinite regress of "what if?" logic loops.

The Frame: At the senior government level—whether you're serving as an ambassador, on the National Security Council, or negotiating between U.S. government agencies—you are not paid to make every decision. You are paid to architect the decision system itself. That means deciding what must be decided, by whom, under what conditions, and compressing everything else into executable logic that moves without you. This is not new, only undernamed. What computer scientists call reduction, military planners call doctrine, and diplomats call standing guidance. All are forms of logic compression—where complex decision trees are collapsed into actionable, reusable formulas. This isn't glamorous. It's plodding, recursive, boring, and vital. It's logic architecture under real-world pressure.

Hypothetical: Symbolic Compression at the Ambassador's Desk

A cable hits your desk: A host nation unit—trained and funded by U.S. security assistance—may have helped smuggle contraband. There's grainy video. The country team is spinning up. Washington will wake up in an hour or less and will be calling; you must have some answers.

Uncompressed Stack: At full fidelity, it's dozens of pages long. But your job is to compress it.

Conditions (C):
- C_1: Two embassy sections confirm the footage is credible
- C_2: Host government delays or denies wrongdoing
- C_3: Value of contraband < \$50K and first offense
- C_4: Public leak occurs before internal report finalized
- C_5: Election year in host country

Actions (A):
- A_1: Pause security assistance, pending review
- A_2: Escalate to interagency with legal matrix
- A_3: Delegate to law enforcement sections with 24-hours to report
- A_4: Initiate no-fault press deconfliction call

Compressed Logic:

- $C_1 \rightarrow A_1$
- $C_2 \wedge C_5 \rightarrow A_2$
- $C_3 \rightarrow A_3$
- $C_4 \rightarrow A_4$

You've just transformed a swirling 30-variable crisis into four deterministic triggers. That is compression. You don't re-ask these questions every time. **You codify the logic once, and run it like software.**

Diplomatic Logic Compression Doctrine

Decide how decisions will route, *before* the crisis forces the choice.

Your job isn't to respond faster. Smart leaders don't necessarily respond faster. They build systems that don't ask the question.
- If a decision recurs more than twice → **codify the trigger**
- If Washington gets pulled in every time → **push logic downward**
- If it risks policy collapse → **elevate only signal**

This is executive clarity. You don't scale by being omnipresent. You scale by compressing ambiguity into structure—freeing your judgment for moments that actually matter.

What This Unlocks:
- **Fewer Escalations:** Washington doesn't get dragged into noise. Your system distinguishes noise from signal.
- **Cleaner Judgment:** Executive bandwidth stays unpolluted by trivia.
- **Team Autonomy Without Chaos:** Staff operate within your decision bounds. They don't need permission—they need logic.
- **Credibility:** You become known not for reacting well, but for never needing to.
- **Velocity Without Panic:** In a fast-moving crisis, your team doesn't scramble. It just runs the playbook you wrote when things were calm.

Subtraction Thinking in Practice

Solid logic isn't about being 100% right, 100% of the time. It's about *making fewer wrong moves*. Start by ditching binary thinking. Replace "this is good" versus "this is bad" with conditional logic:

If x, then do y. Otherwise, do z.

This doesn't eliminate uncertainty. It just reduces its power over you.

Don't optimize what feels good; optimize what survives scrutiny. Ask:
- What would falsify this belief?
- Where has this failed in the past?
- What does someone smarter than me think, and why?

If your logic can't pass these tests, it might just be storytelling in disguise.

Strategic Architect Rule

Compression isn't just a cognitive tool; it's how senior leaders survive and thrive. In complex systems, you don't scale by doing more. You scale by doing fewer things at a higher level, because your logic already handled the rest.

In diplomacy, as in all senior leadership, the highest form of decision-making isn't doing more—it's building a structure so precise you almost never have to. When you get really good at it, it'll feel like cheating.

Bonus: Debug Your Day

Most people don't audit their own reasoning. They just keep working harder, assuming output equals value.

Instead: debug.
- What do I keep doing that doesn't add value?
- What patterns do I justify but never inspect?
- What assumptions feel true but have never been tested?
- Where is emotion driving the car while logic sleeps in the trunk?

You don't have to debug your *whole life*. Just pick the top three things that drain your bandwidth daily. Then create a better decision path for each.

Build Your Internal Diagnostic

You already run diagnostics on your calendar, inbox, and gear. Why not your mind?

Start here:
- **Base Rates** – What happens most of the time? (Not what you *hope* will happen.) What's the default outcome for others in your shoes?
- **Opportunity Cost** – What are you giving up by saying "yes" to this? What system is losing time while you defend this one?
- **Second-Order Effects** – If this works, what will it create or demand tomorrow?

If you only remember one thing from this chapter: "Every recursive decision you compress today is one crisis you won't have to solve tomorrow."

You don't scale by doing more, you scale by deciding once, cleanly, and never again.

Good logic is boring. That's why it's powerful. It trades charisma for clarity. Style for substance. Delay for decisiveness.

Before you say "yes," ask what it costs. Before you repeat, ask whether it failed, and if so, why. Before you escalate, ask what your real goal is. That's logic. And it pays dividends forever.

Clarity Beats Effort and Systems Beat Stress

Replace busywork, inbox chaos, and meeting bloat with execution clarity and leadership systems that scale.

The 72-Point Font Ultimatum

I was once part of a team trying to get a stalled joint initiative off the ground. It had been briefed. Endorsed. Nodded at. But nothing moved. Every meeting ended with some new procedural excuse—another form, another review, another delay.

So I changed tactics.

At the next meeting, I walked in with one PowerPoint slide. Just one. No details. No arguments. Just a single sentence in 72-point font:

I can't fund this unless you sign within three days.

You see—I was the bank.

I controlled the financial mechanism that made the entire effort real. And by turning that mechanism into a deadline, I created a forcing function no one could ignore.

They signed the next day.

Not because I raised my voice. Not because I had better facts. But because I stripped the situation down to two variables that always get results: time and money.

That's what Subtraction Systems do. They remove ceremony, performance, and fragile persuasion. They replace them with operational clarity. With levers.

Directive communication. Task/condition/standard formatting. Backbriefs. These aren't soft skills. They're hard tools. And when you use them precisely, you don't need escalation—you just need alignment.

Chapter 1: Negotiation Bandwidth – Winning Without Burning Bridges

Win-Win Wins the Day

Core Problem

Some people treat every negotiation the same: like a battle. But not every negotiation has to be a fight. It's not always zero-sum and not every win looks like a discount. The best negotiators know the real goal isn't victory; it's bandwidth. The smart ones reclaim it through better timing, better tactics, and better framing, whether they're dealing with a used car salesman, an angry coworker, or a stubborn Prime Minister.

Elastic vs. Inelastic Negotiations
Every negotiation falls somewhere on a spectrum between **elastic** and **inelastic**.
- **Elastic negotiations** are with people with whom you'll keep working: bosses, coworkers, kids, spouses, or long-term partners. The relationship matters. So does your reputation. You don't win by squeezing, only by creating durable agreements that preserve momentum and goodwill.
- **Inelastic negotiations** are one-time events: car purchases, real estate deals, tourist market haggling, vendor bids, even buying a company. You likely won't see them again. The outcome matters more than the optics.
- *Author's Note:* I know that there are other definitions for elastic / inelastic negotiations, but I like these.

Knowing which type you're in dictates how you reclaim bandwidth.

Systems / Tactics – Elastic Negotiations

1. **Reclaim Bandwidth by Framing Shared Outcomes**
   People are more flexible when they see the upside. Instead of pushing for a lower price or shorter deadline, reframe your ask around mutual wins:
   - "If we can agree on this timeline, I can commit extra bandwidth to your other priorities."
   - "If I take this on, I'll need to shift something else; can we talk about what matters most?"

   This isn't bluster, it's structural alignment.
2. **Leave Them Room to Say Yes**

Never back someone into a corner in elastic negotiations. Bandwidth dies when people feel trapped. Give options, even if one is clearly better.

- o "Would it help if I took x off your plate?"
- o "We can move on y, or adjust z, but not both. What's best for you?"

3. **Build Equity Before You Spend It**
Trust is a bandwidth bank. Show up early, bring something to the table first, deliver reliably, and the other party will extend more flexibility. You're not negotiating from scratch; you're negotiating on interest you already earned.

4. **Use Silence, Not Force**
People talk to fill silence. That includes revealing their true bottom lines. In elastic settings, measured silence isn't rude; it's strategic. Pause. Let the offer settle. They may sweeten the deal just to avoid an awkward silence.

5. **Context Shift as a Reset Tool**
If you're hitting friction, shift the context:
- o Time: "Maybe we try again next week?" (people eager to move forward might balk at this)
- o Stake: "Let's step back—what's really driving this?" (why are you the way that you are?)
- o Authority: "I can bring in [authority figure] if it helps clarify scope." (the equivalent of the car salesman getting his manager)

Shifting context reframes the terms without direct confrontation.

6. **The Red Team Rehearsal**
Before any high-stakes meeting, rehearse the opposing side's logic:
- o What do they fear?
- o What are they willing to lose?
- o What deal would they hate but still accept?

This 10-minute mental exercise cuts hours of friction later. If you can anticipate, you don't have to react.

Systems / Tactics – Inelastic Negotiations

1. **Pre-Anchor*, Then Counter**
You control the terrain by setting the first number. If they beat you to it, respond with a counter based on credible comparisons.
- o "Other units with similar mileage are $3,000 lower."
- o "We've seen vendors offer this scope at 25% less."

Anchoring reclaims bandwidth before the real conversation starts.

> * This has a downside as well, however, if your first number is wildly different than theirs. Too high and they can walk away. Too low and you've left money on the table. It also gives them insight into your mindset. Knowing which strategy to employ is an art.

2. **Kill Friendly Fluff**
In inelastic deals, niceties cost time. Be direct, stay polite, and treat friendliness as noise unless it's functional. You're not trying to build rapport; you're trying to optimize terms.
- o The exception to this is if you think the cost of rapport is worth it.

3. **Use Walkaway Power**
The biggest bandwidth comes from being able to say no. If your deal isn't time-bound, signal that you're not desperate:
- o "This is helpful. I've got a couple others I'm comparing; I'll let you know."

- "I'm looking for value here, not just speed."

A clean walkaway resets the terms. Use it sparingly, but always be willing.

4. **Force Movement with Asymmetry**

   If they won't move on price, shift the conversation:
   - Add-ons: free accessories, support, or upgrades
   - Payment terms: delayed billing, better financing
   - Time value: faster delivery or priority handling

   Even in zero-sum settings, you can find angles to extract value.

5. **The BATNA Stack** (this deserves its own book, FYI)

   Before you walk into any deal, know your BATNA—your Best Alternative to a Negotiated Agreement. And upgrade it:
   - Can you line up a backup vendor?
   - Can you delay the decision with minimal cost?
   - Can you make your fallback path visible?

Your BATNA is your bandwidth reserve. The stronger it is, the cleaner you negotiate.

Strategic Architect Rule

In elastic negotiations, protect the relationship. In inelastic negotiations, protect your terms. Either way, your job is to reclaim bandwidth—time, money, or mental clarity—without creating friction.

Vignette: Maybe the Real Win Was the Relationship We Made Along the Way

In one high-stakes negotiation, I sat down with foreign officials to secure backing for a joint initiative. Another team had handled early discussions and built strong momentum and they had an excellent relationship with the interlocutors. I was brought in late—as the funding lead—to close the deal.

Our ask was ambitious: deep, tangible investment from our partners, not just signatures. I laid out the logic, the structure, and the shared benefits. It wasn't cheap. But it made sense.

And they said yes.

That wasn't luck. That was bandwidth: credibility, preparation, and a framework rooted in trust. The result? A faster launch, cleaner execution, and long-term cohesion across the team.

Bandwidth ROI Table – Negotiation

Type	Bandwidth Target	Tactic	Time Saved	Value Created	Risk if Mishandled
Elastic	Relationship + long-term trust	Shared outcomes, soft framing, optionality	Ongoing	Compounded trust, smoother ops	Burned relationships, resentment
Inelastic	Price, terms, immediate ROI	Anchoring, walkaway, asymmetry	Hours to days	Thousands in cash/time	Lost deal or bad terms

Final Note

You can't negotiate well if you don't know what kind of game you're in. Elastic deals require finesse. Inelastic deals require edge. Either way, bandwidth is the hidden win.

Reclaim it or leave it on the table.

Chapter 2: Leadership by Fire, Tactical Command for Civilian Life

Shoot, Move, Communicate

Tales From the Field – Rules to Fight By

Before one of my closest friends left for USMC Officer Candidate School, I did what any decent friend and former rifle platoon leader would: I built him a playbook. Not doctrine. Not theory. Just something that would keep his head clear when things got weird.

But I didn't build it alone. I started necessary movement: I called in fellow veterans who had led in combat, failed under pressure, and rebuilt after. What emerged was a blunt, no-BS survival document: Rules to Fight By.

The Commander's Intent for the document was to put everything we wished someone had handed us on Day One:
- What to do when you're in charge but untested
- How to manage people who know more than you
- When to shut up, when to step in, and when to carry the full weight of failure
- What power is and how to apply it

The point wasn't inspiration. It was operational survivability.

Because when the bandwidth evaporates, when someone's bleeding out in a ditch, when a deal collapses in front of a client, or when your team locks up under pressure, your intent doesn't matter. Your inputs don't matter. Only clarity, command presence, and system ownership matter.

My friend carried the playbook into Officer Candidate School. And I've carried it into embassies, startups, crisis response teams, and family systems. It works because it's not built for theory; it's built for fire.

Core Problem

Civilian leadership training (books, keynotes, corporate seminars) is often optimized for perception, not performance.

Why?

Because in non-lethal, low-friction environments:
- Charisma scales faster than competence
- Risk is reputational, not operational
- Leadership is performative, not mission-critical

So, the guidance shifts accordingly:
- Focus on how you're perceived, not what you deliver
- Soften your language to maintain psychological safety (even when urgency is required)
- Spend more energy maintaining likability than enforcing standards

Civilian Leadership Focus

Civilian Advice Focus	Why It Dominates
Likability	Feedback culture, peer influence
Tone coaching ("I feel...")	Corporate HR priorities outweigh clarity
Motivational fluff	Easy to sell, harder to measure
Abstract models	Allows ambiguity, avoids accountability
Executive presence	Often code for aesthetic/charismatic polish

What It Misses

Real leadership isn't aesthetic. It's operational.

When crises arise—supply chains breakdown, legal jeopardy, PR collapse, active shooter, family emergency—command presence matters more than being approachable. Soft framing and vague requests collapse under pressure.

Civilian frameworks teach you how to *seem* in charge.
Military frameworks teach you how to *be* in charge, especially when everything breaks.

Summary

Civilian leadership culture rewards:
- People who look like leaders out of central casting
- People who speak like facilitators
- People who prioritize consensus over clarity

But clarity is what keeps people alive under pressure, whether that pressure is literal fire, financial collapse, or reputational fallout.

You don't need to be liked, though it does help and managing that balance is its own book. You do need to be understood, trusted, and obeyed without confusion.

The Tactical Leadership System below is a distillation of the collective 47 years of service of six dudes who have seen the elephant.

Tactical Leadership Systems

1. Don't Ask; Do Tell

"Don't ask a subordinate to do something. Tell him."

Directive clarity is not rude; it's respectful. It removes ambiguity and protects time.
- Bad: "Can someone maybe take a look at this if time allows?"
- Good: "Sarah, please resolve this with Finance and brief me by 1500."

This isn't about tone. It's about bandwidth. Every soft ask requires interpretation. Every incorrectly interpreted order introduces latency and friction.

2. Intent Is Everything

Task. Condition. Standard. (TCS). TCS conveys the Commander's Intent.

Every action you request, verbal or written, should answer:
o   Task: What needs doing?
o   Condition: What are the limits or resources?
o   Standard: What does "done right" look like?

Confused teams don't need better people. They need better leaders.

3. Lead Before You're Liked

"You'll grow close to your men. But they are not your friends. Not until one of you is out."

Civilian version: Rapport isn't authority. You're not here to be popular. You're here to create momentum, alignment, and results.

Respect comes from consistency, clarity, and follow-through. Not drinks at happy hour (but that does have its place).

4. Own Everything Below You

"I am responsible for all my unit does or fails to do."

o   If they're undertrained, that's on you.
o   If a document's missing, that's on you.

o   If morale drops, that's on you.

Know where every task, person, and dollar is. If you wouldn't tolerate sloppiness in a combat unit or home, don't tolerate it in your team. "The standard you walk past is the one you accept."

5.   Up the Chain, Down the Chain

Command is bidirectional.

o   Up: Don't report problems without proposed solutions.
o   Down: Never bypass your mid-levels or Non-Commissioned Officer equivalents. You weaken the chain when you cut through it.

Always report, even when no one asks. Even if there are no answers, give an update. If your boss is blindsided, you didn't lead. Bosses hate surprises.

6.   Be Visible. Be Loud. Be First (except at mealtimes).

Command by spreadsheet doesn't work; you have to be there to lead.
o   Jump into the friction zones.
o   Use your command voice.
o   Be the first one in, and the last one out (but leaders eat last and they carry their own bags)

Leading from the front still matters. So does presence.

7.   Challenge = Respect

"Tell your troops it can't be done and watch them outpace your best estimate."

Comfort kills momentum. If your team is cruising, they're drifting. Challenge them, sharpen them, reorient them.

Raise the bar. Then raise it again.

8.   Leadership: Built, Not Born

When someone says, "He's a born leader," what they really mean is "He has charisma." Charisma isn't leadership. It's theater.

Louder for those in the back: CHARISMA IS THEATER, NOT LEADERSHIP.

Charisma might get you the mic. It might win you the room. But when the pressure hits, things go sideways, the team fractures, the mission stalls, or the literal bullets are flying, charisma doesn't hold the line.

Systems do. Clarity does. Relationships do.

Real leadership isn't something you radiate (but you can cultivate gravitas, which is its own book). It's something you construct. Built through friction: You don't become a leader by being admired. You become one by being tested.

Earned through clarity: People don't follow noise. They follow direction, presence, and purpose.

Enforced with consistency: Trust compounds only when your standards don't move.

The civilian world rewards charisma, style, posture, presence. The real-world rewards competence, systems, judgment, and trust under fire.

ROI Table: Leadership Systems That Protect Bandwidth

Subtraction System	Minutes Saved Daily	Hours Saved Yearly	Days Saved Lifetime	Annual Value	Lifetime Value
Directive Communication	12	52	108.3	$2,600	$130,000
Task Clarity (T/C/S format)	9	39	81.3	$1,950	$97,500
Up/Down Chain Integrity	6	26	54.2	$1,300	$65,000
Delegation with Ownership	12	52	108.3	$2,600	$130,000

Chapter 3: Supervision That Creates Bandwidth

How to Lead Without Hovering, Fix Without Micromanaging, and Scale Without Burning Out

Core Problem

Many managers supervise like they're still responsible for every micro-output. They hover, check, second-guess, and wonder why they're burned out. I refuse to do any of that, as long as everyone produces. If a star performer is done with their tasks for the day and wants to leave an hour early, why do I care? If a steady worker who always gets her stuff done wants to work from home, that's great; enjoy not having a commute.

But someone who wants to micromanage all that?

That's not leadership. That's drag.

Supervision isn't about watching people work. It's about building a system that runs without you.

Systems / Tactics – Leading for Autonomy, Not Attention

1. Trust Is a Multiplier

Every person you trust to execute without follow-up buys back:
- Check-in time
- Correction loops
- Emotional bandwidth
- Goodwill from the employees

This is how managers go from three direct reports to 30 without going numb.

Strategic Architect Rule
If you can't walk away for 24 hours without a fire, you don't have a team, you have well-paid liabilities.

2. Clear Commands = Bandwidth Upfront

Supervision breakdowns are front-loaded.
Most failures start with:
o   Vague tasking
o   No success criteria
o   No ownership pathway

Fix it at the beginning stages by using this simple directive structure.

Command Format:
I need **[x task]**, by **[y time]**, in **[z format]** from **[persons responsible]**.

If **[contingency]** happens, what will **[persons responsible]** do?

Set task, condition, standard, deadline, and require a backbrief.

3. The Five-Minute Backbrief Rule

After every major task:
o   "Tell me your next step."
o   "What happens if it breaks?"
o   "What are you waiting on?"
o   "Do you need anything from me (guidance, information)?"
This takes five minutes. Saves five hours.

4. Trust, but Track

Micromanagement isn't accountability.

Instead, supervise your **systems**, not your **people**.
o   Use dashboards
o   Set targets on the calendar; use these benchmarks to compare current status to the desired outcome
o   Only intervene if green turns yellow

If you can't see the system, you're guessing.

5. Correct Once. Document Twice.

Don't chase the same problem over and over. Create a repeatable policy:
o   **First time:** coach it
o   **Second:** document it
o   **Third:** retrain or remove
The goal isn't punishment; it's consistency. You're protecting everyone's time.

Three Modes of Delegation

Delegation isn't a single tool; it's three. Systems break down not because people are lazy, but because the wrong kind of delegation was used for the task.

Delegation Mode	Description	Use When
Authority Transfer	You assign a decision and its outcome to someone else.	The person is capable and empowered to act alone.
Ownership Enforcement	You assign a task, but retain command oversight.	The task is complex or strategic; requires supervision.
Mechanical Offload	The task is handed to a machine, system, or automation tool.	It's repetitive, time-based, or doesn't require judgment.

Strong leaders use all three. Weak ones default to #2, hovering under the illusion of delegation.

Supervision ROI Table

Subtraction System	Minutes Saved Daily	Hours Saved Yearly	Days Saved Lifetime	Annual Value	Lifetime Value
Backbriefs (daily tasks)	5	21.7	45.1	$1,083	$54,167
Autonomy systems (less checking)	5	21.7	45.1	$1,083	$54,167
Error reduction (via T/C/S clarity)	10	43.4	90.2	$2,166	$108,300
Fewer unnecessary meetings	15	65.1	135.3	$3,249	$162,450

Chapter 4: Email & Messaging

Batching, Templates, and Automation – How to Kill the Pings Without Losing Control

Tales From the Field

I once tracked every email I sent in a week: 312 messages (a light week). Only 28 required original thought. The rest? Scheduling, confirming, forwarding, thanking, or rewriting things I'd said before.

Each message felt fast, two minutes here, five there. But by Friday, I'd lost nearly eight hours. A full day gone to the least valuable kind of work: responding.

I don't remember the last time I scheduled a meeting manually. Or filtered a promo email. Or rewrote a standard reply from scratch.

That's not because I'm lazy. It's because I built the system once.

Core Problem

We treat email and messaging as if they're urgent by nature. They're not.

We treat each message like it's bespoke, when most are just templates waiting to materialize.

We confuse *responsiveness* with *productivity*, and *inbox zero* with *control*. In reality, every unbatched check of your inbox, every retyped reply, every missed automation is a bandwidth leak.

Automation isn't about replacing people. It's about reclaiming **bandwidth**.

Systems / Tactics

1. **Template Libraries and Canned Replies**
   - Build a personal library of your most used replies.
   - Subject lines, intros, and signoffs should not be invented twice.
   - If you've sent it more than twice, template it.

2. **Batch Email and Messaging Windows**
   - ○ Check your inbox two to three times a day.
   - ○ Disable notifications. Pop-ups are saboteurs.
   - ○ Slack and Teams are inboxes in disguise; batch them too.
3. **Scheduling Links**
   - ○ Use automated online scheduling systems. Doesn't matter which one.
   - ○ Stop burning six messages to find a meeting time. Drop a link and move on. If someone can't meet at that time, they are free to propose another.
4. **Use Smart Tools** (yes, even ChatGPT)
   - ○ Draft memos, summarize transcripts, generate outlines, scaffold Standard Operating Procedures (SOPs).
   - ○ Let the machine write the first draft; you edit and own the second.
5. **Email Filters & Auto-Archives**
   - ○ Kill promo spam. Auto-sort newsletters.
   - ○ You should never see an email you didn't ask for.
6. **Write Shorter Emails**
   - ○ Five sentences or less.
   - ○ If it takes more, it probably shouldn't be an email; it should be a quick call.
7. **Protect Deep Work Windows**
   - ○ Mornings are for thinking, not thanking.
   - ○ Calendar it like a meeting. Don't apologize for doing real work.

Strategic Architect Rule

Inbox zero is a trap. *System zero* is the win. The goal isn't to be a better responder. It's to *need fewer responses* in the first place.

ROI Table: Email & Automation Time Saved

Subtraction System	Minutes Saved Daily	Hours Saved Yearly	Days Saved Lifetime	Annual Value	Lifetime Value
Email templates & canned replies	5	21.7	45.1	$1,083	$54,167
Fixed inbox check windows	7.5	32.5	67.7	$1,625	$81,250
Messaging app & email batching	5	21.7	45.1	$1,083	$54,167
Scheduling links	2.9	12.6	26.2	$628	$31,417
Email filters & auto-archive	2.1	9.1	19	$455	$22,750
AI task automation	4.3	18.6	38.8	$932	$46,583

Closing Argument

Every email you send manually, every time you retype what could be copy-pasted, every ping you respond to on someone else's schedule, it's all drag. Not because you're bad at email. But because your system isn't doing the work for you.

Let the systems think, so you don't have to.

Chapter 5: Next-Level Bandwidth – Digital, Financial, Social, and Mental

Focus on the Small Stuff

Tales From the Field – The Bandwidth of Bandwidth

People focus on the large-scale ROI reclamations: commuting, emails, meetings. But **real mastery happens in the quiet doors and corners**: the background systems, the digital defaults, the headspace no one audits.

I learned this the hard way: deploying, managing international affairs, raising a kid, running a business. When things got tight, it wasn't the hours I planned that saved me. It was the ones I reclaimed from the bandwidth of bandwidth.

Core Problem – Digital Hygiene

Your phone is not your friend. **It's a system breach.**

Phones don't just waste time. They fracture focus, hijack attention, and burn decision cycles on junk input. **They're dopamine slot machines, and unless you reprogram them, they'll run your life.**

Systems / Tactics – Reclaiming Control

Turn Off Notifications
- No banners
- No badges
- No sounds
- No pop-ups
- **Default = silent**

Only exceptions: calendar alerts, calls, emergency contacts.

Home Screen = Tools Only
Your home screen is your **mission loadout**.
Apps allowed:
- Calendar (work and family)

- Notes
- Calculator
- Maps
- Phone / Text
- Clock
- Camera
- Virtual Meeting App

Everything else: buried in folders, off-screen, or deleted. If it's not operational, it's not visible.

Set Email Windows

You don't need to check email all day. You run a trapline.

- Morning scan – 15 minutes
- Afternoon reply block – 30 minutes
- Batch responses
- Use canned replies + filters
- If it's important, they will

Social Media Firewalls

Social isn't evil, but it must be caged.

- No social apps on your phone
- Browser-access only if absolutely needed (adds friction)
- Set a hard timer
- Log out after every session

Do Not Disturb = Default

You are not open 24/7. You are on mission.

- Use Focus Modes
- Silence during deep work, family time, workouts, sleep
- Emergency bypass for key people only

Audit the Feeds

Your attention is a finite asset. Every scroll is a budget decision.

- Unfollow. Unsubscribe. Declutter.
- Use RSS or curated sources
- Limit to three trusted* news inputs
- No autoplay; no endless scrolls
  *Media literacy and critical thinking are other major issues that deserve their own books.

Airplane Mode = Bandwidth Reset

Airplane Mode isn't just for flights. It's for clarity.
Use it during:

- Writing
- Planning
- Problem-solving
- Deep conversations
- Other high-cognitive tasks
- Workouts

ROI Table – Digital Discipline Bandwidth

Subtraction System	Minutes Saved Daily	Hours Saved Yearly	Days Saved Lifetime	Annual Value	Lifetime Value
Notification shutdown	3	13	27.1	$650	$32,500
Email batching	9	39	81.3	$1,950	$97,500
Social media controls	10	43.3	90.3	$2,167	$108,333
Focus/Do Not Disturb use	5	21.7	45.1	$1,083	$54,167
Feed audit	0.5	2.2	4.5	$108	$5,417

Strategic Architect Rule

Digital hygiene is time discipline. The more you declutter your inputs, the more power you retain for real work, real decisions, and real peace. If your phone runs your schedule, your mood, and your mind, you've already lost. Reclaim the bandwidth. Lock down your inputs. Focus your attention like it matters. Because it does.

Digital Audit – Strip It Down

At week's end, ask yourself:
- How many inputs hit your brain this week?
- How many were necessary?
- How many were noise?

Then:
- Unsubscribe
- Delete apps
- Limit to core functions
- Set Do Not Disturb defaults
- Your phone works for you now, not the other way around

Chapter 6: The Calendar Is a Kill Zone

The Calendar Is Lying to You (and to Congress)

On paper, you've got time. But paper doesn't last long in the real world.

Tales From the Field – You Think You Have 10 Days. You Have Three.

That deliverable you've got due in 10 calendar days? Monday starts late because you're flying back from Cabo. Wednesday, you're chaperoning your kid's field trip. Thursday's a federal holiday. Friday you're off-site.

That "10-day" window? You're down to four now. **It's not bad planning; it's calendar illusion.**

Even Congress falls for it.

The U.S. House of Representatives technically meets year-round. But once you subtract weekends, federal holidays, district work periods, recess, foreign travel, committee-only days, and ceremonial business, the actual number of legislative working days is shockingly small.

Congressional Calendar Illusion Table (U.S. House)

Category	Days
Total days per year	365
Weekends (52)	-104
Federal holidays (10)	-10
District work periods / recess	-60–75
Committee-only / non-Floor days	-40–50
Travel, events, ceremonial sessions	-20
Actual Floor legislative days	**106–131**

Even the U.S. Congress, backed by 12,000 staffers and trillions in budget, gets only **106–131 meaningful working days per year** for real legislative activity.

The rest is calendar noise: appearances, obligations, optics, and gridlock. Now look at your own calendar. You think you've got 10 days?

Sidebar: Calendar-Driven Failure Modes

You don't run out of energy. You run out of room.

These are real examples of what happens when calendar illusion wins:
- **Missed Appropriations:** Key bills die because the Floor schedule collides with recess. If markup isn't done by August, it's dead by October.
- **Lapsed Authorities:** Programs sunset simply because no one blocked time to renew them. Not for lack of support, just lack of priority.
- **Botched Negotiations:** One side runs out of bandwidth. Key negotiators fly out, change assignments, or burn out mid-deal. The clock wins.
- **Last-Minute Crises:** Everyone saw it coming. But no one scheduled time to deal with it. So, it explodes in someone else's inbox.

I've seen multi-million-dollar initiatives get kneecapped by calendar illusion. Everyone thinks they're working from a wide-open runway. Nobody realizes half the runway is underwater.

Core Problem

The calendar is a liar, if you don't interrogate it.

Some people glance at their week and see white space. I see grenades: time bombs waiting to blow-up your focus, steal your momentum, and squeeze your bandwidth.

Congress doesn't get a say in much, but it obeys the calendar. Legislative recesses, markup timelines, and Floor schedules are built on one thing: blocks. If it's not on the calendar, it doesn't happen. If it *is*, it gets priority.

Your life is no different. If you don't own your calendar, you don't control your output.

Systems / Tactics

1. **Run a Weekly Calendar Audit** (Sunday or Friday PM)
   - Identify *frag days* in advance: travel, events, family obligations, burnout/health breaks
   - Look for days that feel open but *aren't*, then plan accordingly
2. **Color-Code by Category**
   - Meetings = red
   - Deep work = green
   - Admin/logistics = yellow
   - Recovery / flex = blue
   This isn't aesthetic. It's pattern recognition.

3. **The 1/3–2/3 Rule – Protecting Execution Time**
   If you're given nine hours to execute a mission, you take three hours to plan, and you give six hours to your team. This forces velocity. It also creates trust. A slow plan equals a rushed team. A fast plan enables the team to breathe, adapt, and win.
4. **Pre-Block Burnout Breaks**
   o Every three to four weeks, schedule a half-day with zero demands.
   o Don't wait until you're cooked. Protect the bandwidth in advance.

Work From Home Doesn't Save You

Even if you work from home, frag days still happen: childcare gaps, network issues, errand clusters. Your calendar still lies. Audit it anyway.

Calendar ROI Table

Subtraction System	Minutes Saved Daily	Hours Saved Yearly	Days Saved Lifetime	Annual Value	Lifetime Value
Weekly frag day audit	5	21.7	45.1	$1,083	$54,167
1/3–2/3 scheduling rule	5	21.7	45.1	$1,083	$54,167
Burnout breaks (prevented)	10	43.4	90.2	$2,166	$108,300

Intent Briefing Framework (GOTWA): A System for Continuity, Not Ceremony

Originally used by military leaders transferring to another area of operations, a GOTWA is a rapid, no-BS way to communicate continuity intent (differing from TCS or Commander's Intent):

GOTWA: Intent Brief Format

G – Where I'm Going	Be specific. What's your next focus, location, or operational area?
O – Others I'm Taking	Who's going with you, physically or on task?
T – Time I'll Be Gone	When are you back? Set the clock. Remove ambiguity.
W – What to Do if I Don't Return	Backup plan. Who steps in? What fallback system is in place?
A – Actions to Take if Enemy Contact Occurs	If something breaks, who does what? Pre-determine responses.

It's not just for combat.

You can use GOTWA logic in almost any high-friction environment: stepping out of a meeting, leaving a project mid-cycle, or handing off tasks. It covers both contingencies and clarity, ensuring your team knows what's happening, when, and why.

You don't go dark. You leave a breadcrumb trail. This applies in business when you delegate meeting leadership, a client call, or a field visit. Your team should always know the backup plan.

Chapter 7: Cutting Meetings

Cut Early, Cut Often

Tales From the Field – Cancel First. Justify Later.

Every time I take over a team, department, or mission, I do one thing first: I cancel every standing meeting. When I was working as a project manager at the Defense Threat Reduction Agency, my boss (Army Lieutenant Colonel) retired, and I got the big seat.

On day one, I found I had 10 weekly meetings (eight hours, 20% of my work week) pre-scheduled to coordinate project building pathogen detection and destruction capacity in Afghanistan. It wasn't even a question; I cancelled all of them. The project had something like 30 people across six agencies and 12 time zones (from New Mexico to Kabul). Moving forward, I allowed necessary meetings to form organically, resulting in a manageable three per week. The result: the team had more time for real work and so did I.

The meetings that matter will reappear—fast, focused, and purpose-driven. The rest? Gone. No one even asks.

According to Harvard Business Review, 71% of executives rate meetings as unproductive. Every hour saved from one useless meeting is an hour reclaimed for actual progress.[3]

Core Problem

Meetings are expensive. Not just in time, but in attention, energy, and inertia. Most don't exist because they're needed; they exist because they've always existed. *We have always been at war with Eastasia.*

They are calendar squatters. Old relics. Redundant syncs. Ancient artifacts. Coordination theater dressed up as productivity.

And because they're recurring, they breed like rabbits.

---

[3] Leslie A. Perlow, Constance Noonan Hadley, and Eunice Eun, "Stop the Meeting Madness." *Harvard Business Review* (July–August 2017).

Systems / Tactics

1. **Delete Every Recurring Meeting**
   o Force re-validation. If it matters, someone will rebuild it, with purpose.
2. **Use Calendar Blocks for Decision Time**
   o Set silent, solo blocks of time to make decisions. No attendees. No discussion.
   o If a meeting requires no decision or deliverable, it doesn't belong on your calendar.
3. **15-Minute Default Duration**
   o Most meetings don't deserve 30 minutes. If it can't be scoped in 15, the issue probably isn't evident.
4. **Write It Down First**
   o Before you meet, summarize the situation in writing.
   o Writing reveals confusion. If it's not clear on paper, it'll be chaos in person.
5. **Use Asynchronous Updates**
   o Daily standups? Project check-ins? Use email, Slack, or dashboards.
   o Meetings are for *decisions* and *friction removal*, not recitations.
6. **Treat Internal and External Meetings Differently**
   o Internally, be lean and async.
   o Externally, be respectful but strict: clear agenda, goal, and owner, or it doesn't happen.
   o (The above is a very important distinction.)

Meeting Disobedience ROI Table

Subtraction System	Minutes Saved Daily	Hours Saved Yearly	Days Saved Lifetime	Annual Value	Lifetime Value
Cancel recurring meetings	6	26	54.2	$1,300	$65,000
Async updates	6	26	54.2	$1,300	$65,000
15-minute default duration	10	43.3	90.3	$2,165	$108,250

Chapter 8: Hotkeys Speed as a System

The Faster You Can Plan, the Faster You Can Execute

Tales From the Field – He Used the Mouse. I Used the System.

I once watched an older gentleman format a four-row Excel spreadsheet like he was defusing a bomb:

Clicking "bold" from the toolbar. "Center" from the menu. "Insert row" with a full wrist trip.

It took him 90 seconds. I rebuilt the same table in eight, with hotkeys only. He stared. I moved on.

The average knowledge worker who masters keyboard shortcuts reclaims eight full workdays per year.[4] That's one extra vacation. For free.

Core Problem

Every time your hand leaves the keyboard, you lose momentum. If you're in Word or Excel five hours a day and still using dropdowns, you're *paying a bandwidth tax*, a click at a time.

Systems / Tactics – Speed as Default

The Math of Motion
Each mouse move = ~2 seconds lost. Each 1,000-word document = 100-150 possible actions. That's 3–5 minutes wasted per file. Multiply by 5 docs/day × 250 workdays/year = 25–40 hours gone, doing what a hotkey could do instantly.

Core Hotkeys You Should Know

Microsoft Word (Windows / Mac)
- **Bold / Italic / Underline**: Ctrl/Cmd + B / I / U
- **Find / Replace**: Ctrl/Cmd + F / H

---

[4] Brill, J. (2020). *Time Management Tips That Work.* (Microsoft productivity blog)

- **Insert Comment**: Ctrl + Alt + M
- **Align Left / Center / Right**: Ctrl/Cmd + L / E / R
- **Undo / Redo**: Ctrl/Cmd + Z / Y
- **Save**: Ctrl/Cmd + S
- **Navigate Headings**: Alt + Shift + → / ←

Microsoft Excel (Windows / Mac)
- **Insert Row**: Ctrl + Shift + "+"
- **Delete Row**: Ctrl + "-"
- **AutoSum**: Alt + =
- **Jump to Last Cell**: Ctrl + Arrow
- **Select Column / Row**: Ctrl + Space / Shift + Space
- **Format Cells**: Ctrl + 1
- **Paste Special**: Ctrl + Alt + V

Pro-Level Speed Tactics
- **Command Stringing**: Ctrl + Shift + ↓ → Ctrl + 1 = bulk format in five seconds
- **Ribbon Navigation** (Windows): Alt → H → A → C = center alignment, no mouse
- **Quick Parts** (Word): save reusable blurbs, policy pitches, or closings
- **AutoText Shortcuts**:
    - ;sig = your full email signature
    - ;blurb = your three-line program summary

Bandwidth ROI Table – Hotkey Efficiency

Subtraction System	Minutes Saved Daily	Hours Saved Yearly	Days Saved Lifetime	Annual Value	Lifetime Value
Core hotkeys (Word/Excel)	5	21.7	45.1	$1,083	$54,167
Command stringing / macros	5	21.7	45.1	$1,083	$54,167
Boilerplate shortcuts	3	13	27.1	$650	$32,500

Strategic Architect Rule
Speed isn't flash. It's function. Every wasted second compounds. You're not just formatting documents; you're signaling competence, responsiveness, and precision. Hotkeys aren't nerd tools. They're **professional infrastructure.**

Chapter 9: Bandwidth in Crisis – When Systems Break

Something Always Goes Wrong

Tales From the Field – You Will Get Sick. Your Flight Will Get Cancelled. Something Will Break.

You will hit turbulence, of the literal or life variety. The question isn't *if* systems fail. It's whether you've built enough structure to hold the line when they do.

Core Problem

Most people only build for the plan. The bandwidth comes from what you've built for the *failure of the plan.*

Systems / Tactics – Emergency Bandwidth

1. **5-Minute Fallbacks for Core Routines**
   For every major daily system—hygiene, meals, work, workouts—you need a compressed version that you can use in a pinch:
   o **Hygiene:** facial wipe, floss pick, mouthwash swish
   o **Meals:** protein bar + hydration + electrolyte tab
   o **Work:** notepad + pen + mobile hotspot or cached doc
   o **Workout:** squats, pushups, stretch circuit; no gear needed
   Think: *If I had five minutes and nothing else, how would I keep moving?*
2. **"Go Light" Kit** (always accessible)
   o Duplicate charger + power bank
   o Backup ID and health card (laminated)
   o $100 cash in small bills
   o Protein bar + emergency meds + foldable toothbrush, tiny tube of toothpaste
   o Paper with key phone numbers and contacts
   o High limit credit card
   o Stored in car, backpack, or office drawer
3. **Offline Critical Access**
   o PDF copy of passport, visa, vaccination records, insurance
   o Screenshots of travel essentials: boarding pass, hotel booking

o Downloaded map + key instructions

If tech fails, your prep shouldn't.

4. **Contact Chains That Work Without You**
   o Written phone list: family, neighbor, doctors, emergency contacts
   o Printed instructions: what to do if you're delayed, hospitalized, or unreachable
   o Shared cloud doc with travel dates, key info, emergency protocols

Bandwidth in crisis starts with someone else being able to step in, without guessing.

Crisis Bandwidth ROI Table

System	Time ROI	Stress ROI	Lifetime Value
5-min fallback routines	Prevents collapse	Maintains continuity	Avoids missed days + momentum loss
"Go light" kit in key places	Immediate relief	High confidence	Removes friction during disruption
Offline critical access	Saves hours	Avoids tech reliance	Rescues key moments without connectivity
Contact redundancy	Outsource-ready	Reduces panic	Enables help to arrive without delay

Strategic Architect Rule

You don't rise to the occasion. You fall to your systems. And when your systems break, your backup systems had better not rely on memory, power, or luck. What you build in calm is what protects you in chaos.

Chapter 10: Commute & Transit

We Don't Care if You're Fast or Slow; Just Show Up and Move

Tales From the Field – Active Commuting

In many cities, driving 3.5 miles during rush hour takes longer than you'd like to admit. Round-trip, it could add up to 20-45+ minutes each day. Over the course of a year, you could be burning 260 hours—*6.5 weeks of your life*—sitting in traffic, sedentary and stuck.

There's a cleaner play: replace your commute with movement. You were going to run anyway. Now that run gets you somewhere.

I run 1,000 miles every year and have done since 2012. When I was posted to Latvia, I ran to work through snow, slush, rain, and sun. Three-and-a-half miles each way. I kept a rotation of non-iron shirts, suits, and ties in the office. I'd shower in the gym, change, and start the day sharper than anyone who just climbed out of a car. Most mornings I had a podcast going: news, language, or absurd deep dives into obscure history. I wasn't "finding time to train." I was solving two problems with one system.

Biking hits the same target. Faster than running, same transit freedom, and easier on your joints. Toss panniers or a backpack on, and you've got a rolling wardrobe and grocery hauler. Bonus: you never look for parking again.

Walking counts, too. When I worked at the U.S. Mission to the U.N. in New York, the subway took just as long as walking. So, I walked, 2.5 miles a day. I got my steps in, listened to podcasts, and kept my transit budget at zero. Every trip was a small win. Over the course of a year, those wins compound into bandwidth.

Commuting via running, biking, walking—they're all optional. But if you live within range, even two days a week will shift your time math and your energy. You're not adding effort. You're replacing a low-value task (driving) with a high-return one (movement).

Core Problem

Physically active commuting is one of the most powerful time-saving combinations in the book. It allows you to exercise and get to work simultaneously. Add in audio learning, and you've just tripled your ROI.

Systems / Tactics

If your circumstances prohibit physically active commuting, transform your commute by using public transit time to plan your day, unwind, or level up your knowledge. Or mix and match your active commute with a morning subway trip followed by an afternoon jog home. Mission (and mileage) accomplished.

The below tables show your ROI if you replace the subway or a car with physically active commuting. All tables assume Manhattan rush hour, 130 days a year (not 260 normal business days) to account for fatigue and weather.

Replacing the Subway ROI - Time Breakdown

Method	Round Trip Distance (mi)	Subway Time* (min)	Commute Time Saved (min)	Exercise Replaced (min)
Walk	2	34	0	34
Run	6.2	65	9	56
Bike	12.4	75	7	68

Subway times vary by commute method, because longer subway routes include added travel time, transfers, and fixed walk-to-station overhead.

Replacing the Subway ROI - Time and Money Saved by Replacing Exercise

Method	Annual Time Saved (hours)	Annual Fare Saved	Annual Value	Lifetime Time Saved (days)	Lifetime Value
Walk	73.7	$754	$3,683	153.5	$184,167
Run	121.3	$754	$6,067	252.7	$303,333
Bike	147.3	$754	$7,367	307.3	$368,333

Replacing the Car ROI - Time Breakdown

Method	Round Trip Distance (mi)	Drive Time (min)*	Commute Time Saved (min)	Exercise Replaced (min)
Walk	2	33	−1	34
Run	6.2	66	10	56
Bike	12.4	90	22	68

Drive times vary by commute distance—short trips get crushed by stoplights and congestion, while longer drives often cover more miles per minute once you hit open roads.

Replacing the Car ROI - Time and Money Saved

Method	Annual Time Saved (hours)	Annual Car Cost Saved	Annual Value	Lifetime Time Saved (days)	Lifetime Value
Walk	71.5	$2,658	$6,233	149	$311,650
Run	143	$2,779	$9,929	297.9	$496,450
Bike	195	$2,958	$12,708	406.2	$635,400

Car Cost

These figures use conservative estimates based on capped daily costs for operating a car in Manhattan:
- Parking: $10/day (yes, I am aware this is really cheap)
- Insurance + loan payments: $10/day
- Gas: calculated per trip (based on distance, $4/gallon, and 18 mpg city)

This means each driving day carries a baseline cost of ~$23–26, depending on trip length. Actual costs may be higher due to:
- Premium parking rates (often $25–$75/day)
- Insurance surcharges for city driving
- Vehicle depreciation
- Tolls and vehicle maintenance
- Congestion charges and other costs

These tables are extremely conservative and intentionally understate the true savings of replacing a Manhattan car commute with walk, run, or bike transit.

Bonus: Movement + Learning = Stacked Output

1. **Listen During Your Commute, Workout, or Ride**
   - Podcasts, language apps, or audiobooks
   - Absorb nonfiction, policy, interviews, or immersive language
   - Passive input while you drive, walk, or train
   - Over the course of a year, that's **90–140 hours of audio learning** with no time cost
   - If you work out 3x/week for 45 minutes, you add 117 hours of mobile learning capacity annually
2. **Making Calls**
   - I make all my calls jogging or in the car. Living overseas as much as I have, you need to take time to reconnect. With a full plate, an hour-long easy run or a half-hour commute provides the perfect opportunity to catch up with friends and family.

ROI: Movement Learning

Subtraction System	Minutes Saved Daily	Hours Saved Yearly	Days Saved Lifetime	Annual Value	Lifetime Value
Commute audio learning	30	130	270.8	$6,500	$325,000
Workout audio learning	15	65	135.4	$3,250	$162,500

SECTION III: *First Routines*

Start Frictionless; Stay Focused

Build a low-drag life by structuring mornings, clothing, and gear that move with you, not against you.

The Systems That Built a Company

When I launched my first product, the Jammock*, a patented, specially designed hammock for Jeep Wranglers (and now Ford Broncos), I didn't have staff, venture funding, or time (I mean, I still don't, but whatever). What I had was a full-time job and a commute. So, I built systems to hold the line. An FAQ for customers. A pre-sale to generate revenue before committing. Leveraging friends to test it. A contractor to build it and another to store and ship it. It wasn't slick, but it scaled.

First Routines are how you apply this mindset to your mornings. Every bit of hassle after you wake up—every delay, every decision—drains your energy before the day even starts. And every messy night sets a trap for tomorrow. But if your morning runs smoothly, with no hang-ups or wasted thought on things like finding clothes or tying shoes, you begin with momentum, and it carries you forward.

The Jammock has generated over $1,200,000 in sales revenue. Not because I worked harder. Because I didn't have to keep touching everything.

Chapter 1: Why Admiral McRaven Was Wrong About Making Your Bed

For Real, It's Dumb. Sir.

Tales From the Field

The morning isn't a ceremony. And here, we don't stand on ceremony, or even have many, unless they serve a tangible function with a real ROI.

Instead, the morning is a launch sequence.

At basic training, beds had to be made tight. Hospital corners. Bounce-a-quarter standards. Every morning. Here's what I did: I only pulled open one of the hospital corners at lights out. I'd slide in and out of bed like it was a sleeping bag, preserving the crisp, untouched look. Result? I didn't spend three minutes re-making my bed every morning. I rolled out, smoothed the pillow, tightened one crease, and was inspection-ready in 60 seconds. Time saved: approximately two minutes per day times 120 days of basic training and Military Police School equals four hours. Mental bandwidth saved: priceless when sleep deprived.

Every repeated action either costs you time or returns it. Strategic Architects don't build routines for symbolism. They build them for velocity. For frictionless flow. For operational momentum by zero six hundred.

Core Problem

Admiral William McRaven famously said, *"If you want to change the world, start by making your bed."*

That's ridiculous ... sir.

Making your bed doesn't change your day. But what you do in your first 30 minutes? That changes everything.

Systems / Tactics

If you want to win the day, don't waste your precious time on dumb rituals.

This chapter is the *philosophical inversion* of Admiral McRaven's bestselling advice. It's not about tidiness. It's about velocity and getting up and doing the things that need to be done.

Obviously, we don't reject discipline—far from it; we repurpose it. Strategic Laziness is disciplined. But it doesn't fetishize effort for the sake of effort. Rather, it eliminates waste and redirects that time elsewhere.

The Methodology: Friction Audit + Functional Design

Ask two questions about every morning task (well, every task, really):
- Does this need to be done at all?
- If yes, can it be simplified, shortened, or eliminated?

Discipline is not now and never has been the goal. Execution without friction is.

The Sacred Cows We Kill Here

Some rituals survive not because they work, but because no one stops to question them, like the dehumidifier spigot or because a four-star Admiral said so.

But we do. We question everything. Our mantra:

We do not stand on ceremony—we put our foot on its neck.

Tying ties every morning. Making beds no one will see. Ironing shirts that never needed to be wrinkled in the first place. These are not signs of discipline. They're signs of drag.

Tying Ties

Most men tie and untie their ties daily. That's two manual actions, 260+ times a year.

Strategic Architects? Tie once. Leave it tied. Use the slip-off method. I have ties that haven't been untied since the Clinton Administration. I am not kidding.

Not "lazy." Efficient.

In the fall of 2000, I moved from Buffalo to Washington, D.C. to intern at the White House. It was the first time I had to wear a tie every day.

I'm an Eagle Scout. I can tie a bowline, a square knot, half hitches, even a blood knot. But I couldn't tie a necktie to save my life. And in 2000, there was no YouTube to bail you out.

So, I did what any efficiency-minded 20-year-old would do: I tied it once—just once—and I never untied it again.

I'd slip it over my head in the morning and cinch it tight. At night, I'd loosen it, hang it, and put it at the end of the rotation. No re-tying. No mirror struggles.

That was the genesis of saving 90 seconds a day before I even knew time had value. Twenty-five years later, I still use that system.

Sidebar: Slip-On Protocols – Micro Systems That Pay Out Daily

Slip-on systems are tiny time savers that *compound every single morning.* They're not hacks. They're deliberate removals of resistance.

Simple Protocols to Save You Precious Morning Minutes

Item	System
Tie	Tie once. Never untie. Loosen, slip over your head, hang, repeat.
Shoes	Use elastic no-tie laces or slip-on dress shoes. No retying; no bending.
Shoehorn use	Eases your foot into your tied shoe; no bending
Belt	Use ratchet belts (e.g. Anson, SlideBelts). Fast click, perfect fit.
Badge/Lanyard	Keep it clipped to your go bag. Never search for it.
Laptop bag	Keep it pre-packed and pre-zipped. Pick up and go.

Itemized Slip-On Protocols ROI Table (260 tasks per year)

Subtraction System	Minutes Saved Daily	Hours Saved Yearly	Days Saved Lifetime	Annual Value	Lifetime Value
Slip-on tie	1.5	6.45	13.5	$325	$16,250
Shoes (pre-tied or slip-on)	1	4.3	9	$217	$10,833
Shoehorn use (speed + no bending)	1	4.3	9	$217	$10,833
Belt (ratchet-style, fast adjust)	0.3	1.1	2.3	$54	$2,708
Badge/Lanyard (ready & reachable)	0.5	2.2	4.5	$108	$5,417

Strategic Architect Rule
If it touches your routine **every day**, optimize it once; then let it run. Saving five minutes a day equates to **more than a thousand hours** of your life, gained without even trying.

Making Beds

No one sees it. No one pays you for it. It doesn't launch your day. It's a visual comfort at best. In basic training, I came up with a better system: sleep under the blanket without un-tucking it. Bed stays (mostly) made. Mission proceeds.

Unless she's coming over (and she cares) skip it.

ROI Morning Savings – Skip Bed-Making

Subtraction System	Minutes Saved Daily	Hours Saved Yearly	Days Saved Lifetime	Annual Value	Lifetime Value
Skipping bed-making	2	8.6	18	$434	$21,667

Tales From the Field – Shaving Time Without the Razor Burn

You're late. Your bag's half-packed. You're digging through drawers for the good razor or that one bottle of whatever actually works on your face. You forget deodorant, or you lose the cap to your toothpaste, and it leaks. Now you're not just behind; you're annoyed, less sharp, and friction is already winning.

I don't do that anymore.

Because I stopped treating grooming like a daily surprise. I systemized it.

Core Problem

People waste minutes each day, and compound hours per year, on grooming logistics they've already solved a thousand times. The problem isn't hygiene. It's friction. Decisions, repacking, missing tools, inconsistent setups.

Systems / Tactics

1. Standardize your tools and sequence.

Use the same razor, toothbrush, floss, hair product, etc. Every time. No improvisation. It's a grooming kit, not a dinner buffet.

Here's an extremely small example that shows how powerful Subtraction Systems are. Buy toothpaste with a flip top, not a screw top. This is a decision that takes zero time to make and removes unnecessary friction. It saves three to four seconds twice a day and you'll never lose the top down the drain, never cross thread it, never fumble, drop, and lose it, wasting more time when it rolls under the vanity and you have a plane to catch.

Do the math: six to eight seconds of extra time, every single day, and no need to ever pay a plumber $100 and spend half your day waiting for him to show up to fish an errant cap out of your pipes.

Subtraction System	Minutes Saved Daily	Hours Saved Yearly	Days Saved Lifetime	Annual Value	Lifetime Value*
Flip-top toothpaste	0.1	0.4	1.4	$33	$2,438

The real value here is not losing the cap or dropping it down the drain, ever, which can be expensive.

2. Duplicate your loadout.
Set up identical grooming kits in four locations:
o   Home base
o   Work/gym locker
o   Car: travel bag (pre-packed and sealed)
o   Go bag

3. Never unpack your grooming kit.
Buy the extras once, and you'll never scramble again. This turns packing into walking out the door.

ROI Table – Grooming Kit System

Subtraction System	Minutes Saved Daily	Hours Saved Yearly	Days Saved Lifetime	Annual Value	Lifetime Value
Standardized grooming kit	1	4.3	9	$217	$10,833

Mental ROI
o   Lower stress
o   Higher momentum
o   More wins before 0700
o   A system that launches you, not one that drags you

Strategic Architect Rule
This isn't laziness. It's deliberate efficiency. Strategic Laziness is ruthless about what moves the mission, and what doesn't. Making your bed doesn't win the day. Momentum, ROI, and substantive work does.

We do not perform order or discipline, we design it.

Tales From the Field – Bookend Your Day Like a Strategic Architect

When I wake up, I don't check email. I don't check Slack. I drink water. I move. I look at the three things that matter most that day. Then I go.

At night, I write down tomorrow's primary priorities, the *Top 3*, lay out my gear, and drop every mental tab into a notebook. Then I sleep.

Why? Because chaos loves an unclaimed boundary. And your most valuable boundaries are your first 30 minutes and your last 30.

Core Problem

Your morning and evening are for setting and resetting your *operating tempo*.

Lots of folks hit the pillow with open tasks and wake up in reaction mode. If you start your day in someone else's inbox and end it in your own, you're not leading your time; you're being led by it.

Systems / Tactics

Morning Flow Tactics

- **Wake up at the same time, even on weekends.**
  Circadian rhythm doesn't care what day it is.
- **Drink water before anything else.**
  Caffeine is not hydration. Email is not oxygen.
- **Move your body.**
  Doesn't have to be a workout, just move.
- **Don't open your inbox.**
  You're not there to react. You're there to execute.
- **Review your day's Top 3 priorities.**
  Use Effort, Leverage, and Impact (ELI) scoring. Don't aim for quantity; aim for compounding outcomes.

Evening Shutdown Tactics

- **Set out gear/clothes for the next day.**
  Kill morning friction before it wakes up.
- **Write down tomorrow's Top 3.**
  Predetermine what matters while your mind is clear.
- **Do a brain dump.**
  Everything that's pinging around your head? Write it down. Reduce sleep latency. Let your mind go quiet.
- **No phone in the bedroom.**
  Leave it outside the room or silence it. You're not the night shift.
  Get a real alarm clock, lol.

Morning & Evening ROI Table

Subtraction System	Minutes Saved Daily	Hours Saved Yearly	Days Saved Lifetime	Annual Value	Lifetime Value
Morning ramp-up (friction reduction)	5	21.7	45.1	$1,082	$54,120
Evening shutdown (better prep & sleep)	5	21.7	45.1	$1,082	$54,120

Every minute shaved off your morning routine isn't just time saved—it is bandwidth reclaimed. By eliminating daily friction points, you're not simply trimming the fat; you're deploying a 10-minute workday savings system that delivers a 43.4-hour annual advantage, translating to 2,165 hours over your career and a lifetime value of $108,240. In layman's terms, that's the force multiplier your day needs to win before 0700. Remember: Strategic Laziness isn't about taking shortcuts; it's about building an operation that runs so smoothly, every second counts.

Strategic Architect Rule
Win the bookends (mornings, evenings). The rest follows. Your inbox doesn't deserve your first breath. Your pillow doesn't deserve your unsorted thoughts. Lead your day by designing its entry and exit.

Strategic Architect Interlude

Not all tasks are equal, but most people treat them like they are (insert obligatory: "when everything's a priority, nothing is").

The Daily Top 3 isn't about doing more. It's about choosing the right three (say it with me): *priorities.*

This scoring matrix filters what earns your focus based on Effort, Leverage, and Impact. If it doesn't move the needle, it doesn't make the cut.

Daily Top 3 – Effort, Leverage, and Impact (ELI) Subtraction Protocol

Priority Item (examples)	Effort (1–5)	Leverage (1–5)	Impact (1–5)	ELI Score (L × I ÷ E)	Notes
Prep brief for senior level meeting	2	5	5	12.5	Reuseable template, high-visibility meeting
Schedule annual medical appointment	1	1	4	4	Low leverage but long-term health ROI
Decline redundant meeting	1	4	3	12	Saves time weekly; resets boundaries

Scoring Guide:
- **Effort (E):** Time, complexity, mental and emotional energy required
- **Leverage (L):** How many other things this unlocks or cascades into
- **Impact (I):** Strategic importance or consequence of completion

How to Use It:
1. List your Top 3 most important tasks for the day
2. Score each for Effort, Leverage, and Impact
3. Use the formula: **(Leverage × Impact) ÷ Effort**
4. Prioritize high-ROI tasks, not just the loudest ones
5. Complete the task with the highest ELI score **first**

How is this different from the Eisenhower Decision Matrix (EDM)?
For those of us who were not subjected to endless briefings on Eisenhower's tool, the EDM is a simple 2×2 grid that helps you decide what to do, delegate, delay, or delete, based on the urgency and importance of a task.

	Urgent	Not Urgent
Important	Do Now	Delay and Plan
Not Important	Delegate	Delete

The Difference

The Eisenhower Matrix helps you triage tasks based on urgency and importance, which is essential for staying afloat in reactive environments. The ELI Subtraction Protocol, by contrast, evaluates actions based on effort, leverage, and impact, allowing you to eliminate low-ROI work and build systems that scale. Eisenhower helps you manage chaos; ELI helps you escape it.

Chapter 2: Time Blocks Are Not Fungible

Batching Multiplies Effects

People think they have a time problem. They don't. They have a blocking problem.
You can save 90 minutes a day, but if that time is scattered across 12 interruptions, it is almost unusable.

Time is most valuable when it's consolidated into larger blocks of itself. Not just saved.

The Time Fragmentation Fallacy

There's a common but false assumption:

"If I save 10 minutes here and five minutes there, I've saved 15 minutes."

Mathematically: true.

Functionally: useless.

A 5-minute block has limited utility. It's just long enough to check email, get distracted, or do a shallow task. It's not enough to think strategically, solve a real problem, or create something that matters. 10-15 minutes? Getting better, but not enough for real, substantive work.

But if you had that same 15 minutes merged into a 60-minute block, paired with the 45 you lose to inbox noise, meeting bloat, or poorly stacked routines? Now you have margin that matters.

The Cost of the Reset

Task-switching costs aren't just theory. It takes the average knowledge worker a substantial amount of time to refocus after an interruption. Dr. Gloria Mark has studied digital distraction for more than two decades. In a 2008 interview cited by Fast Company, she noted that the average knowledge worker takes about 23 minutes to return to a task after being interrupted, a figure widely referenced in productivity literature (though not published in a peer-reviewed paper). While I think 23 minutes sounds excessive and is likely dependent on the person, I will defer to the experts. Her broader research, including "The Cost of Interrupted Work: More

Speed and Stress," confirms that interruptions lead to faster, more error-prone work and elevated stress levels.[5]

That means if your attention is reset six times a day, you're burning 2.5 hours just trying to return to your original task. Not actually doing the work, just returning to it.

The block is the asset. Not the time.

Morning Stack: Building the First Block

Nowhere is this more obvious than your morning routine. If you save two minutes here or three there, you can reclaim a 20–30-minute block before the day even starts, a block that can be used for reading, planning, exercise, writing, or getting out the door earlier to avoid traffic.

How to Reclaim Your First Real Block

Subtraction Stacks That Create the Morning Launch Block

System	Minutes Saved
Don't make the bed	2
Use default wardrobe / prep the night before	3
Slip-on shoes	1.5
Badge/key staging	1
Set up coffee/hydration the night before	5
To-go / go-to breakfast	2
Default to-go lunch	4
Other multitasking	3
Total	**21.5**

Net effect: 22-minute block by 7:30 a.m.

The Block Multiplier

Block Size (min)	What You Can Do	ROI Range
15	Reply to email, reschedule something	$5–10
30	Review goals, do real prep, run 3 miles	$25
60	Deep work, writing, systems	$50–150
90	Strategic planning, hard problems	$150–500+

---

[5] Gloria Mark, Daniela Gudith, and Ulrich Klocke, *The Cost of Interrupted Work: More Speed and Stress*, in *Proceedings of the SIGCHI Conference on Human Factors in Computing Systems* (New York: ACM, 2008), 107–110.

Larger blocks aren't more valuable just because they're longer. They're more valuable because they unlock activities that can't fit in smaller blocks.

Use It, Or It Disappears

Blocks that aren't protected are eaten. If you save 30 minutes and then give it back to Instagram, email drift, or indecision, you haven't won anything.

Blocks are how you build systems, recover energy, think clearly, and escape urgency. They're not a reward. They're a requirement. Don't just save time. Stack it. Every system in this book gives you back time. But that time is only valuable if you amalgamate it into blocks large enough to be used for work that matters.

Scattered minutes provide convenience, but consolidated hours create capability.

Sleep Multiplier

Time saved in the morning isn't just about getting out the door faster or collapsing into bed sooner; it's about reclaiming the block that sleep requires for effectiveness. Sleep isn't fungible in 20-minute chunks. It's a system that compounds when uninterrupted and breaks down when fragmented. By stacking low-effort subtractions you can win back 20 to 30 minutes of bandwidth that can be given to sleep. And that's a high-ROI trade. More sleep sharpens focus, lowers reactivity, increases willpower, and reduces decision fatigue the next day. One reclaimed block of sleep powers every other system in the book.

If you scoff at my Subtraction Systems that save a minute here or 90 seconds there, look again. They're not small in the aggregate. They can add up to a significant nightly sleep credit, which pays dividends in energy, focus, and better decisions every single day.

Chapter 3: Fast Gear Systems

Take Care of Your Gear and It Will Take Care of You

Tales From the Field – Everything You Carry Should Save Time or Prevent Failure

I once missed a key meeting because I packed the wrong charger. Not because I was lazy, but because I didn't have a system.

(wrong charger => phone died => couldn't check Outlook calendar => missed meeting)

After that, I packed a full charger setup into every bag I used: daypack, laptop bag, go bag. The problem never recurred.

Soldiers never go into battle without Sergeants performing precombat checks. Likewise, returning from a patrol, you top-up your vehicles with fuel, clean weapons, and reup your ammo, making sure everything is ready for the next mission.

Lesson learned: **Everything you carry should save time or prevent failure.**

If it doesn't, it's dead weight.

Core Problem

If your gear isn't buying you time, it's costing you. Your loadout shouldn't reflect preference. It should reflect function. Forget minimalist or maximalist; you need functionalist.

Every item you carry should reduce decisions, increase readiness, and remove friction. That's it.

Core Kit – Systems You Carry Every Day

1. **Pre-Packed Laptop Bag**
   o Charger, adapter, mouse, USB key, clicker, backup earbuds
   o It lives packed. You never "get your gear together."
   o Outcome: Zero prep time, zero forgotten tech
2. **Default Daypack Loadout**

- Lip balm, pen, phone charger, mints, ibuprofen and any essential meds (EpiPens, anyone?), wipes, headphones, and any other necessities
- One lives in your car, one in your office, one in your go bag
- You reload it, not restock it
- I keep a spare workout loadout (shoes, shorts, etc. in my car in case the mood strikes me)

3. **Slip-On Gear Protocols**
   - Tie once; never untie
   - Ratchet belt, pre-tied shoes with a shoehorn
   - Badge on lanyard always clipped to your bag
   - *Each one removes a micro-delay that compounds daily*

4. **Shoes That Don't Make You Think**
   - I once bought a nice pair of dress shoes that couldn't grip an icy sidewalk; what good were they in the winter?
   - What if you absolutely must run or perform basic evasive action? Can your high heels do that?
   - Can you walk three miles, run to a gate, stand for hours, walk through a puddle? If not, your shoes are dead weight in disguise.

Sustainment Kits – Systems That Eliminate Repeat Buys

1. **YETI-Style Water Bottle**
   - Insulated (cold water tastes better), rugged; get a carry strap for it and throw a carabiner on it (have you ever been somewhere and thought to yourself "man, I really couldn't use an extra carabiner here"?)
   - You fill it. You carry it. You never buy plastic again.
   - $300/year saved, plus zero thirst-driven detours.

2. **Reusable Shopping Bags**
   - Stashed in trunk or bag
   - Avoids fees, clutter, and last-minute detours
   - Useful for more than just groceries
   - Better for the environment

3. **Rechargeable-Only Systems**
   - Use rechargeable batteries or devices with internal lithium cells
   - Label and rotate. Never run dead. Never buy AAAs at a hotel kiosk again.

Gear & Repeatables ROI Table

Subtraction System	Minutes Saved Daily	Hours Saved Yearly	Days Saved Lifetime	Annual Value	Lifetime Value
Pre-packed laptop bag	1	4.3	9	$217	$10,833
Default daypack loadout	5	21.7	45.1	$1,083	$54,167
Slip-on gear (tie, belt, shoes)	5	21.7	45.1	$1,083	$54,167
Decision-proof footwear	5	21.7	45.1	$1,083	$54,167

Reusable shopping bags	1	4.3	9	$217	$10,833
Rechargeable-only systems	1	4.3	9	$217	$10,833

Tales From the Field – The Last Water Bottle I Ever Bought

For years, I bought bottled water out of habit. $2 here, $3.50 there. Airports, gas stations, cafeterias—never thirsty, but always paying for it.

Then I bought a YETI 38-ounce insulated bottle. This one-time purchase holds more water and keeps it colder than any plastic bottle. I fill it before I leave the house and stop thinking about it. I ditched the screw-top cap, bought the flip-top cap (saves 3-5 seconds per use), and a bottle sling (carry strap for the bottle), converting my water bottle into an easily transportable hydration center. The sling also has a zippered pocket and adds a bit more R-factor (R-1?) to YETI's already robust thermal insulation. Useful.

It paid for itself in fewer than two weeks.

Hydration ROI Table

Subtraction System	Minutes Saved Daily	Hours Saved Yearly	Days Saved Lifetime	Annual Value	Lifetime Value
Reusable water bottle (YETI)	1	4.3	9	$215	$10,750
Cost avoided (bottled water)	(N/A)	(N/A)	(N/A)	$520	$26,000

Strategic Architect Rule

If it touches your day, it should never slow it down. Your gear should make you faster, sharper, and harder to knock off rhythm. Otherwise, it's just clutter disguised as preparedness.

Chapter 4: Decision-Free Clothing

Merino Systems – Travel Light, Dress Sharp, Move Faster

Tales From the Field – Rome, Wool, and One Italian Compliment

At the start of the pandemic, I traveled to Rome for a professional exchange on security policy.

The airline lost my luggage.

I hadn't packed a suit in my carry-on, so I landed with nothing but the clothes on my back: an Icebreaker Merino long-sleeve shirt, Lucky Brand jeans, and Keen Voyageur boots.

Not exactly peak diplomatic form. And Rome isn't where you want to show up underdressed—especially not at a ministry building where even the janitor dresses like a Milan runway extra (he doesn't, but Rome lends itself to that kind of exaggeration).

The next morning, I walked into the meeting still wearing the same outfit. About forty people gathered in our working group. I stood, introduced myself, and apologized for the field-casual look.

A senior Italian delegate cut me off:

"Not at all. I think you look sophisticated and smart."

Coming from that man, in that building? That was the green light. I've trusted Merino ever since.

"You'll see I wear only gray or blue suits [author's note: or tan, lol]. I'm trying to pare down decisions. I don't want to make decisions about what I'm eating or wearing. Because I have too many other decisions to make."

— Barack Obama, on minimizing decision fatigue[6]

Core Problem

---

[6] Barack Obama, quoted in Michael Lewis, *Obama's Way*, Vanity Fair, October 2012, https://www.vanityfair.com/news/2012/10/michael-lewis-profile-barack-obama.

Many travelers and professionals fall into one of two traps: overstuffed or underfunctional.

Every extra piece of luggage costs you time, energy, and options. Every friction-laden garment bleeds effort. Most people pack to feel prepared. Strategic Architects preload and run lean.

Your gear should:
- Survive a 10-hour flight
- Pass in a business (or diplomatic) meeting
- Handle a long walk to the airport gate
- Dry overnight on a hanger
- Still look sharp the next morning

I'm not saying you shouldn't also throw a suit in your carry-on, but if you follow these tips, you'll be well-prepared.

System – Merino Wool + Capsule Travel

Merino isn't luxury (I mean, it *is* soft, wrinkle and odor resistant, and you barely need to wash it). It's **mission gear**.

Merino base layers collapse travel, fitness, and formal wear into a single, breathable, antimicrobial, wrinkle-resistant system. It's your go-anywhere kit, without the ironing board.

Travel Tactics:
- Replace three to four shirts with one or two Merino base layers
- One on, one washed; overnight hang dry
- Packing cubes for modular systems (sleep / work / workout)
- Carry-on only (if you can swing it!)
- Capsule wardrobe = no outfit changes, no backups

System – Charles Tyrwhitt Shirts + Merino Wool Suits

The daily version of the same logic:
- Charles Tyrwhitt non-iron dress shirts = machine-washable, hang dry, no ironing, no dry cleaning
- Merino suits = wrinkle-resistant, odor-resistant, breathable, durable
    - Rotate weekly, brush lightly, steam as needed
    - Dry clean two to four times per year, not after every wear. In fact, don't by dry clean only clothes unless you absolutely must. Tuxedos, dresses, etc. are caveats.

Travel & Wardrobe ROI – Time Efficiency

Subtraction System	Minutes Saved Daily	Hours Saved Yearly	Days Saved Lifetime	Annual Value	Lifetime Value
No checked baggage	0	1.5	3.1	$75	$3,750

Avoided baggage fees (2x a year)	0	0	0	$150	$7,500
Packing/unpacking time saved	0	5	10.4	$250	$12,500

Wardrobe ROI – Dry Cleaning and Ironing Cost Comparison

Subtraction System	Minutes Saved Daily	Hours Saved Yearly	Days Saved Lifetime	Annual Value	Lifetime Value
Iron-free shirt system	3	13	27.1	$650	$32,500
Eliminate shirt dry cleaning (156 × $3)	0	0	0	$468	$23,400
Reduce suit dry cleaning (230 fewer × $6)	0	0	0	$1,380	$27,600
Fewer dry cleaner trips (48 fewer × 30 min)	5.6	24.3	50.6	$1,213	$60,667

Sidebar: Merino Suit Loadout – Buy Once, Rotate (Almost) Forever

The System (Professional Edition)
- **Suits:** Five Merino wool suits (navy, charcoal, mid-gray, subtle check, dark blue)
- **Rotation:** Weekly or based on context
- **Care:** Brush, steam, air overnight
- **Dry Cleaning:** two to four times per suit per year (max 20/year)
- **Storage:** Wide-shoulder hangers, garment bags, cedar inserts

Why Merino Wins

Feature	Merino Wool	Standard Suit Fabric
Wrinkle resistance	High – natural resilience	Low – creases easily
Odor control	Excellent – antimicrobial	Poor – absorbs and traps odor
Breathability	High – thermoregulating	Low – traps heat
Durability	Long-lasting if maintained	Shorter lifespan
Cost efficiency	Higher upfront, lower lifetime	Lower upfront, higher turnover

Projected ROI – 20-Year Outlook

Factor	Cheap Suit Grinder	Merino Loadout
Cost per suit	$300	$900
Suits needed	50	15
Total suit cost	$15,000	$13,500

Dry cleanings/year	260	30
Dry cleaning cost/year	$1,560	$180
20-Year dry cleaning cost	$31,200	$3,600
Total wardrobe cost	**$46,200**	**$17,100**

Cognitive ROI
- Reduced stress
- Faster transitions
- Sharper appearance with less effort
- More room for mission-critical decisions

Strategic Architect Rule
One shirt that handles airport sprints, policy sit-downs, and hotel workouts without a wash? That's not luxury; it's a force multiplier. Merino isn't fashion. It's frictionless readiness. You're not dressing up. You're loading out.

Chapter 5: Pre-Packing

They've done studies, you know. 80% of the time, it works every time.

Tales From the Field – The Kit Is the Mindset

In the military, packing isn't just about gear, it's a reflection of the mindset of the packer. Every item in your ruck or suitcase has a cost: in weight, in volume, in time spent organizing and rechecking.

I learned early that *the best soldiers don't just pack lighter; they pack smarter.*

The best kit I ever built didn't evolve during a deployment. It was ready before the call. A go bag that was already dialed-in and pre-loaded, with critical gear in familiar places. I didn't think about what was in it. I already knew.

Core Problem

If you're rebuilding your travel or deployment kit from scratch every time, you're burning bandwidth.

Reactivity isn't readiness.

A true Strategic Architect maintains a go bag like a sidearm: *prepped, repeatable, frictionless.*

Systems / Tactics – Pack Like a Professional

1. **The Pre-Packed Go Bag**
   o **Duplicate toiletries:** toothbrush, floss, deodorant, lip balm, etc. (liquids in a TSA-ready clear quart-sized bag)
   o **Rolled compression layers:** socks, underwear, shirts, etc.
   o **Comms kit:** dual chargers, battery pack, plug adapter, wired earbuds
   o **Hygiene module:** wipes, sanitizer, etc.
   o **Essential medications:** ibuprofen/acetaminophen + any prescriptions that you'd be in a bind without

- Admin kit: pens, waterproof notebook, copies of ID/passport, paper with key contact info
- Miscellaneous essentials: $100 in cash (small bills), protein bar, water

Every item earns its place. No last-minute loadouts. **Grab bag. Zip. Go.**

2. **Pack by Function, Not Category**

Civilians pack for trips like they're folding laundry: shirts with shirts, socks with socks. It's neat, but it's slow and stupid.

- Your pack-by-mission module:
- **Sleep kit**: eye mask, earplugs, socks, hoodie (practical for covering head for sleeping on the go or on airplanes)
- **Hygiene kit**: packed in a.m./p.m. order of use
- **Base layers**: three-day clothing module, pre-staged
- **Mission kit**: laptop, USB, notepad, reference docs

Each module should be **a snap-in component**. You can extract it, deploy it, and reset it in seconds.

3. **Deployment Setup**

When on mission, I always do the following to avoid losing stuff in the churn[7]:

- **Arrange room in zones**: sleep, gear, admin, hygiene
- **Staging shelf**: prep next-day gear the night before
- **Most important gear**: on the bedside table or desk (phone, passport, wallet, badge, ID, laptop etc.)
- **Unpack fully only if staying >5 days**

Every system reduced friction and saved **hours** over time. No more digging. No more re-sorting. No more wondering if you packed the cable.

ROI Table – Field Packing & Deployment Bandwidth

Subtraction System	Minutes Saved Daily	Hours Saved Yearly	Days Saved Lifetime	Annual Value	Lifetime Value
Pre-packed go bag, Function-based packing, Deployment setup, Reduced forgotten items	2	8.6	18	$434	$21,667

Strategic Architect Rule

If you pack from scratch, you're not ready. You're just lucky you had time. Packing is thinking. Your kit reflects your mindset. *Live light. Move fast. Stay operational.* The more friction you remove from your gear, the more bandwidth you reclaim in your life.

---

[7] "The Churn" (from James S.A. Corey's "The Expanse") refers to the unpredictable cycles of chaos and instability that wipe out plans, power structures, or people, especially for those at the bottom. When the churn hits, it doesn't care who you are. It resets the board. Strategic Architects don't fight The Churn; they build systems to weather it. "The Churn" deserves much more than the short shrift I give it here, but this book isn't about that.

Chapter 6: Standardized Grooming

Selling Is Like Shaving; if You Don't Do It Every Day, You're a Bum

Tales From the Field – Brush, Rinse, Think

I don't remember when I started keeping mouthwash in the shower. Probably around the same time I realized I was brushing my teeth while pacing the kitchen.

Now my morning routine looks like this:
- Step in the shower
- Brush teeth and use mouthwash (while getting wet)
- Wash body
- Shave while conditioner works
- Mentally review my top three tasks for the day
- Dry off and walk out already a step ahead

That's not multitasking. That's **task stacking**, where the overlap is physical, not mental. No quality sacrificed. No time wasted. Subtraction systems that stack aren't multitasking; they're designed to avoid the cognitive penalty multitasking creates. In true multitasking, your attention splits between two tasks that both demand focus—like answering email during a necessary meeting. But stacking isn't that. Stacking pairs one high-effort task (like running) with low-effort companions (like listening to a podcast or commuting). There's no quality loss, because only one task requires real attention; the others ride along. Subtraction stacks preserve attention while multiplying output.

Core Problem

Hygiene tasks are required. But that doesn't mean they need to be *separate*.

If you're still brushing, flossing, rinsing, shaving, and showering in serial order, you're giving away **10–15 minutes a day** for no gain.

And while your body goes through the motions, your brain could be doing something better than just counting shampoo pumps.

Systems / Tactics – Hygiene, Movement & Cognitive Stacking

1. **Mouthwash in the Shower**
   - Rinse while you soap. Spit at the drain.
   - Same result. One less trip to the sink.
2. **Pee in the Shower**
   - You're an adult. The water's running. Just do it.
   - No judgment. Just efficiency.
3. **Meditate or Mentally Rehearse While Showering**
   - No phones, no screens; perfect time to run your "Top 3" list or rehearse a conversation.
   - Mental bandwidth builder.
4. **Brush While Walking**
   - Great during kid wrangling or house patrol.
   - If you're not spitting into a trash can by the stairs at least once a week, are you even optimizing?
5. **Shave in the Shower** (Mirror Optional)
   - Steam keeps your pores open, cleanup is instant, and time overlap is real.

Hygiene ROI Table

Subtraction System	Minutes Saved Daily	Hours Saved Yearly	Days Saved Lifetime	Annual Value	Lifetime Value
Shower + Mouthwash + Pee	1	6.1	12.7	$304	$15,208
Shave* + Shower	2	12.2	25.4	$608	$30,416

Shaving in the shower stacks tasks during passive time, such as conditioner set or rinsing.

Strategic Interlude: Time Value of Systems – Why Starting Early Matters

You don't just save time when you optimize daily routines; you gain compounded advantage.
- One hour saved at age 20 isn't the same as one hour saved at 50
- At 20, you can reinvest that hour 30,000 more times
- At 50, your runway is shorter, your energy is taxed, and your bandwidth is thinner
- Just like money, time compounds when you invest it early

If you build these systems in your 20s or 30s, you're not just getting more done; you're building a lifetime time dividend that pays out every single day.

The ROI of brushing your teeth in the shower isn't just 90 seconds; it's 90 seconds × decades × whatever you use that freed time for.

Strategic Architect Rule

The younger you start saving time, the more that time is worth. That's not theory; it's temporal economics. Optimize now and compound forever.

Chapter 7: Sleep, Recovery, and Food

The Foundation Upon Which Life Happens

Tales From the Field – Recovery Is Operational Readiness

Rest isn't the opposite of performance; it's the enabler of it.

The best operators, athletes, diplomats, and CEOs don't just grind. They recover on purpose. They protect their sleep, fuel with intent, and systemize recovery like it's part of the mission. Because it is.

Core Problem

Too many high performers treat sleep and nutrition as afterthoughts. Too many smart people waste time wondering what to eat next.

You can't execute well if you recover poorly. And you can't think clearly if you're making 21 meal decisions a week.

Systems / Tactics – Recovery and Nutrition That Run on Rails

Sleep Discipline:
- Same bedtime every night, weekends included
- Use a shutdown ritual (30 min of no screens, low light, quiet tasks)
- Red light bulbs in bedside lamps to cut blue spectrum stimulation
- Blackout curtains + white noise = full sensory shutdown
- Sleep in 90-minute cycles (e.g. aim for 7.5 hours, not random durations)
- Use a smart tracker (Oura, Garmin, Whoop) to optimize wake windows

Sleep ROI – Not Just Rest, But Recovery

Subtraction System	Minutes Saved Daily	Hours Saved Yearly	Days Saved Lifetime	Annual Value	Lifetime Value

Better sleep quality (fewer mistakes, faster recovery)	5	30.4	63.4	$1,520	$76,041

Nutrition Systems

Default Breakfast – One Example (feel free to add your own)
- Protein fruit smoothie (add your favorite fruits and a scoop of protein)
- Use a cordless rechargeable blender + (my personal preference) GNC Gold Standard protein (avoid if lactose-intolerant)
- To clean, simply quirt some soap into the blender and fill with water—no delay, no decision fatigue

Prep Three Lunches Ahead
- Protein + veggie + carb
- Stack from fixed grocery template
- Same lunch 3x/week = reduced stress + consistency in macronutrients

Modular Pantry = Meal Assembly, Not Cooking
- Fast fuel stash (no-prep meals):
  - Hard-boiled eggs + cheese stick + crackers + baby carrots
  - Tuna packet + tortilla + orange
- Pantry stocked by macronutrient category:
  - Proteins (cans, powders, pouches)
  - Carbs (instant rice, oats, bread)
  - Fiber (fruits, veggies, seeds)
  - Fats (nuts, oils, avocado)

Meal Planning Logic
- Fixed format with minor weekly rotations
- Decision fatigue gets removed at the source

Nutrition ROI – Time, Energy, and Focus Reclaimed

Subtraction System	Minutes Saved Daily	Hours Saved Yearly	Days Saved Lifetime	Annual Value	Lifetime Value
Default breakfast	4	17.3	36.1	$867	$43,333
Lunch system (3x/week)	2.4	10.4	21.7	$520	$26,000
Modular meal prep	4	17.3	36.1	$867	$43,333

Strategic Architect Rule
Sleep isn't a luxury. Food isn't a variable. They're core systems, not afterthoughts.

You don't squeeze them in; you design around them. What most people burn willpower to manage, you solve once through logistics and repeat. Same outcome. No friction.

Chapter 8: Parenting Bandwidth

The Best Thing That Ever Happened to Me

Tales From the Field – Parenting Is Leadership on a Timer

No one tells you this up front, but so much of parenting is logistics. My son is my best friend; he's ten years old. He was an easy baby, then toddler, and now a young man. My wife, Nadia, and I have moved Alessandro around a lot. He's lived in India, Latvia, Trinidad and Tobago, Washington D.C., and Rochester, NY. We expect a great deal from him and it's not really fair. Regardless, we know what it takes to move a child worldwide and have him thrive.

Parenting is managing gear, food, movement, sleep, communication, and emotions—often simultaneously—with incomplete data and variable terrain, in various locations where you might not have access to that favorite stuffed animal or snack.

It's also the most mission-critical thing you'll ever do. If your systems aren't locked in, your bandwidth disappears fast.

What I've learned: you don't need more time. You need systems that give it back.

Core Problem

Parenting doesn't reward efforts, especially if you fail. It rewards structure.

When you wing it, the day slips. When you prep it, the day flows.

It's not about being a perfect parent. It's about building repeatable bandwidth that lets you be **present** when it counts.

When my son was born, we were in the hospital for five days. Lousy "dad bed," wife in pain, lots of providers coming in for tests, diaper changes, and feedings interrupted so much. Our problem was that we did not have a sleep plan. A simple "you only need one adult on duty at a time" would have helped immeasurably. We had an unspoken agreement that both of us should be awake for each feeding, diaper change, and test. In retrospect, this was stupid. Two adults should be half the work, not twice the work. Our sleep plan was garbage, and we didn't even think of it as a problem until years later. "Amateurs talk tactics, professionals study logistics" was never more in evidence.

Systems / Tactics

1. **Prep the Night Before**
   - Clothes out, lunches packed, bags loaded.
   - Tired-at-night beats frantic-in-the-morning every time.
2. **Visual Systems for Kids**
   - Picture checklists. Color-coded gear bins. Clocks with icons.
   - When they can see the system, they can start owning it.
3. **Parallel Routines**
   - Get dressed while they do.
   - Eat when they eat.
   - Mirror your actions to save time.
4. **Use Parental Taxi Time for Audio Learning or Deeper Conversations**
   - Commute time = kid podcast time. Education doesn't need a classroom.
   - Bonus: both brains get sharper as your kid gets to and from school, sports, or activities.
   - **My pick:** Use the commute to have deeper conversations with your children.
5. **Keep a "Quiet Kit" for Critical Calls**
   - Small bag of books, puzzles, or headphones.
   - For those moments when you need silence but can't disappear.

Parenting Time Savings Table

Subtraction System	Minutes Saved Daily	Hours Saved Yearly	Days Saved Lifetime	Annual Value	Lifetime Value
Night-before prep	4.3	18.6	38.8	$932	$46,583
Visual systems for kids	3	13	27.1	$650	$32,500
Parallel routines	10	43.3	90.3	$2,167	$108,333
Quiet kit (saves reschedules)	1.4	6.1	12.6	$303	$15,167
Audio learning in vehicle	10	43.3	90.3	$2,167	$108,333

Boom, you just saved a year's college tuition (#lolsob).

Conclusion – Living Deliberately

These aren't hacks. They're systems—built with intent, tested under pressure, and refined to eliminate drag. You're not optimizing for novelty. You're engineering conditions where the essentials run cleanly and the noise stays out of your lane.

Every minute reclaimed translates to time for what actually matters. Not some distant day in the future—now, while you still have the clarity, energy, and reach to use it well.

Bandwidth is finite. The discipline is deciding what deserves it.

Strategic Architect Rule
Don't parent on reactivity. Parent on rhythm, structure, and systems that carry the load, so you can carry what matters.

Parenting Bandwidth Case Study

Running isn't just movement. Done right, it's a friction eliminator, cognitive reset tool, and system stacker.

When life gets complex, kids, deadlines, pressure, it's not the perfect gym schedule that saves you. It's a compact, repeatable activity that keeps everything moving.

Field Report – Russian, Fatherhood, and a Jogging Stroller

At the tender age of 37, I was learning Russian at the Foreign Service Institute with a two-year-old at home. Not great with languages. No time. High stakes. If I didn't pass the exam at the end of the year, I didn't just lose my assignment; I risked losing my job. No language proficiency meant no tenure meant no job.

So, I started running.

I'd load my son into the jogging stroller, put on Russian language audio lessons, and go. While I was out, I stuck marketing magnets on every Jeep Wrangler I saw to pitch my side business.

One run. Four outputs:
- Language acquisition (use a speaker, not headphones, so the kiddo can hear too)
- Parenting time
- Entrepreneurship
- Workout

That wasn't multitasking. That was *bandwidth stacking*.

The System – Running as a High-ROI Platform

Bandwidth Reset
- Clears cognitive clutter
- Solves problems in the background
- Resets stress loops

I do my best thinking when I'm running.

Merged Tasking, Not Multitasking
- No travel time or prep friction
- Run becomes:
  - Learning time (podcast at 1.5x)

- o   Call time (check in with family, friends, mentees)
- o   Commute time (run to office, errands, or after school pickup)
- o   Social time (informal run club, training partner, post-run coffee/beer)

"You don't need an hour. You need 20 minutes, a loop, and a reason."

Minimal Input, Maximum Output

- 100–140 calories/mile
- Increases insulin sensitivity
- Improves sleep, mood, metabolism
- Sustains mobility over decades

But more importantly:

- It interrupts the spiral.
- No energy → skip workouts → sleep worse → feel worse → spiral continues.
- One run breaks that loop.

Identity Reinforcement

- You don't run to win. You run to stay consistent.
- Three times per week is enough to stabilize your fitness and self-image.
- Every run is a signal to yourself: *"I will not go gently or quietly."*

Strategic Guidelines

- **Run early.** Before the day gets a vote. (Author's Note: This is more of a "do as I say" moment; my runs usually happen after noon, or near sundown when I am stationed in the tropics.)
- **Don't sprint unless you want to.** You're building bandwidth, not accumulating medals.
- **Repeat routes.** Eliminate planning friction (Author's Note: I found a ½ mile loop in Port of Spain that was well-lit, level, and had some shade. I parked my car next to it and had an aid station every half mile. I did over 1,500 loops.)
- **Don't obsess over metrics.** Just go.

Summary – Why This Works

Running doesn't *take* time. It *gives it back,* layered with other outputs.

- You learn.
- You decompress.
- You parent.
- You reconnect.
- You stay in shape.
- You check things off, without switching contexts.

It's not about athleticism (but it does return that to you). It's about motion as bandwidth.

You don't need motivation. You need a system that makes not-running harder than just going.

Stack what matters. Remove what doesn't. That's not multitasking. That's **strategic architecture.**

Chapter 9: Everyday Carry – Items That Earn Their Place

"The Things They Carried," by Tim O'Brien (a great book about the Vietnam War, check it out)

This is different from Section III: Chapter 3 Fast Gear; I promise.

Core Problem

Everything you carry costs you something: Space. Weight. Attention.

But when you need it, **really need it**, the value spikes instantly. This chapter isn't about survivalist cosplay.

It's about everyday operational readiness for people who move, think, lead, and handle things. What follows is a tiered system:

From **Tier One** (on-body) to **Tier Three** (retrievable within 60 seconds).

You won't carry it all. No one does. But what's on the **menu**. Pick what matches your life, and carry what earns its place.

Tier 1: On You – Everyday Carry (EDC)
Minimum viable readiness. What's always on your body—no bag required.
- Phone (fully charged, key apps updated)
- Wallet or slim cardholder + cash
- Keys (with multitool or tracker)
- Watch (with alarm and health tracking)
- Blister bandage or alcohol wipe (in wallet)
- Emergency meds (EpiPen, inhaler, etc.)
- Chapstick (SPF-rated)
- Microfiber handkerchief
- Pocket knife (legal and functional)
- Lighter (reliable, not decorative)
- Pen or pencil
- Small rechargeable flashlight

- Useful belt (bonus if it doubles as webbing/tourniquet)

Tier 2: Within Reach (Car, Bag, or Desk)
What lives in your backpack, glovebox, or work setup. Used weekly or in minor emergencies.
- Power bank + cables (USB-C, Lightning, micro-USB)
- Mini first aid kit (gloves, gauze, painkillers, wound wipes)
- Anti-diarrheal and pain reliever (travel-grade)
- Spare glasses or contacts
- High-calorie, shelf-stable snack
- Collapsible water bottle
- Notebook + Sharpie
- N95 or KN95 mask (dust, smoke, illness)
- Full-size multitool (pliers, screwdrivers, scissors)
- Emergency cash ($100 in small bills)
- Medium rechargeable flashlight

Tier 3: At Home – Base Layer Resilience
72-hour sustainment + emergency readiness. Stored at home, pre-staged, or easily deployable.
- Expanded first aid kit (shears, tourniquet, burn cream)
- De-choker device
- Jumper cables or jump starter pack
- Water supply + shelf-stable food
- Spare clothes (socks, shirt, underwear)
- Personal defense (pepper spray, legally compliant)
- Utility gloves (tactical or work)
- CPR mask or barrier
- Paracord or ratcheting tie-down straps
- Hard-copy info sheet (contacts, insurance, meds, blood type)
- Pre-packed go bag (modular, ready to roll)
- Portable radio or backup comms
- Paper maps + compass
- Battery-powered lantern
- Large rechargeable flashlight
- Travel documents + digital backups
- Cash reserve ($300–$500)
- Multi-day medication supply
- Water filter straw or purification tabs
- Emergency blanket
- Rugged laptop/tablet with essential files

Strategic Architect Rule
Every item you carry is a bet:

- That you'll need it.
- That it's worth the space.
- That it'll work when it counts.

If it doesn't **save time**, **reduce friction**, or **prevent failure**, leave it behind. If it does? Carry it with confidence and update your loadout quarterly.

Closing Thought

You don't have to carry a mission loadout. You just need to carry **intentionally**. Consider scenarios where 60 seconds means everything. *Gear is bandwidth.*

Chapter 10: Movement and Etiquette – Navigate the World Without Friction

Get Out of Your Way

Tales From the Field – Stop Walking Like a Tourist

You can spot the difference instantly. The tourist stands in the middle of a hallway. Stands in the middle of the escalator and stops at the top. Blocks both sides of the sidewalk. Doesn't know which direction to turn, so they pivot three times and move none.

The professional moves with efficiency. They don't waste steps. They don't block progress. They don't need to think about where to go next; they're already halfway there. Etiquette isn't just about being nice. It's *situational awareness*. It's the discipline of moving through public spaces without becoming a friction point in someone else's day.

Core Problem

Movement inefficiency is invisible bandwidth loss. So is public space friction. We waste time by standing in chokepoints, taking the long way, failing to prep, and drifting through shared environments like they belong to us alone. This isn't about being faster.

It's about *moving without creating drag*, on yourself or others.

Systems / Tactics – Physical and Social Movement That Works

1. **Urban Movement** – Rules of the Jungle (invert for left-side countries)
   o **Escalators:** Stand right, walk left. Always.
   o **Doorways:** Move through them; don't stop to talk, search, or freeze.
   o **Hallways:** Stay right unless passing. Know your footprint.
   o **Crosswalks:** Look left, right, then left again. Don't trust the signal; trust your eyes.
   o **Sidewalks:** Keep right unless passing. Walk with intent. Don't drift. Cut corners when it makes sense.
   o **Phones:** Step aside to check, reply, or navigate.
   o **Public audio:** No speakerphone. No TikTok blasts. Use headphones. For goodness' sake, no one needs to hear your calls/songs/YouTube videos.
2. **Trails and Terrain** – Never Give the Mountain Anything

o Switchbacks preserve energy and reduce injury risk; take them only if they make sense.
o Avoid dips and divots when possible. Going down means you'll pay it back going up.
o Preserve elevation. Preserve spine. Preserve momentum.
3. **Windy Roads and Logic**
o **Cyclists and runners:** Cut apexes when safe and visible.
o Never cross center lines on blind curves.
o Memorize your route: gutters, light cycles, bottlenecks, potholes.
o Lights always on, front and rear, even in daylight.
o Take the lane when needed. Hugging the curb invites accidents.

Vignette – Apex Theory and the Go-Kart Truth

I was recently on a go-kart track with my son. Same karts. Same engines. Same top speed. He should have crushed me since I outweigh him by a hundred pounds.

I got a late start, and he was 50 meters ahead of me. I caught him in three laps. Not because I was faster, but because I was shorter. Every time he swung wide through a corner, I cut the apex on each. Tight lines. Minimal drift. No wasted distance.

Let's call it what it was:
- **8 turns per lap × ~5 meters saved per turn = ~40 meters saved per lap**
- Over three laps? **~120 meters** reclaimed.
- That's more than two full kart-lengths per corner cycle.

He drove with gusto. I used geometry.

What This Unlocks

This isn't about driving. It's about *how you move through constrained systems*: physical, mental, or logistical.

When power is equal, **the geometry you use is leverage.** When speed is relatively constant and capped, the fastest route is the one with **no wasted arc.**

But here are the boundaries:
- In driving, running, or cycling, **cut corners only when it's safe, legal, and visible.**
- In baseball, apexing makes you **slower** because momentum matters more than raw distance. The traditional basepath is 360 feet long, with four sharp 90° turns. But the fastest path isn't the shortest. A smooth, curved route runs closer to 400 feet, adding distance but preserving momentum. That adjustment can cut total time by up to 25%, a potential gain of three to four seconds. Geometry bends to physics. Speed rewards flow, not corners.[8]
- In high-power auto racing? Distance is negotiable. **Exit velocity is king.** Take wide lines to slingshot out of the curve faster than you entered.
- In soldiering? Slow is smooth and smooth is fast.

---

[8] Paul Carozza, David A. Johnson, and Daniel Morgan, *Baserunner's Optimal Path* (Urbana-Champaign: Department of Physics, University of Illinois at Urbana-Champaign, 2010), https://baseball.physics.illinois.edu/BaserunnersOptimalPath.pdf.

Knowing which system you're in is key to maximizing your speed through it. Then cut only what saves time *without losing control.*

Sidebar: The Lane Tax

Want to see how geometry punishes drift in real time? Step onto a standard 400-meter track.

One full lap in Lane 1 is, as advertised, 400 meters.

But Lane 8? Without a staggered start, it's over 453 meters.

That's not a rounding error. That's 13% more distance—53 extra meters—for the same loop, same speed, same start and end point.

Now map that to behavior:
- One extra step on each turn.
- One wider arc per cycle.
- One habit of always drifting instead of cutting.

This isn't metaphor. It's mathematics:
- 1.22 meters per lane $\times 2\pi \times 7$ lanes ≈ 53.7 meters added
- Over 8 lanes, that's a visible tax on anyone who can't or won't stick to the inside line.

In competitive running, staggered starts correct for this. But life doesn't give you one.

If you always take the wide way around—around process, around risk, around the hard edge of the task—you will lose to someone slower who ran smarter.

The shortest legal line is always Lane 1.

You don't need to be faster than everyone. You need to stop running in Lane 8.

Common Track Event Distances by Lane

Lane	200M	400M	1600M
1	200	400	1,600
2	203.8	407.7	1,615.3
3	207.7	415.3	1,630.7
4	211.5	423	1,646.0
5	215.3	430.7	1,661.3
6	219.2	438.3	1,676.7
7	223	446	1,692.0
8	226.8	453.7	1,707.3

Practical Application: Lane Tax, Meet the Stoney Chicane

I've run the Stoney Chicane—a 958-foot segment in upstate New York—more than once. It's a modest stretch of suburban road with a compound curve, invisible to most as anything more than an inefficient jog through a quiet neighborhood.

But on Strava, it tells a deeper story.

At full speed, hugging the apex of each curve, I completed it in 47 seconds, averaging 4:22 per mile. The next closest competitors—talented runners in their own right—took 19 seconds longer on average, even though they were running hard. Why? Because most took the outer line. They ran up to 3% farther—a difference of about 27 feet—simply by staying wide instead of cutting smart.

That 3%? It matters. In performance, it always does. It's the same 3% you save by late-apexing in a go-kart. Or by placing your foot just inside the line instead of outside it. Or by choosing your battles—literally and metaphorically—where geometry favors leverage, not effort.

The go-kart teaches you that life isn't won in the straights. It's won in the corners. The Stoney Chicane confirms it.

Run Commuting and Pedestrian Systems
- Know the route before you launch.
- Make noise when passing; don't run up silently.
- Don't stop in high-flow zones to adjust gear or take selfies.

Efficient Etiquette by Location
Airports
- o Boarding pass ready before the gate.
- o Shoes off, laptop out, liquids prepped before you reach the X-ray belt.
- o Don't clog the jet bridge or hover at the baggage carousel.

Dining and Cafes
- o Know your order before you reach the counter.
- o Clean your tray. Wipe your table. Reset for the next person.
- o Don't linger during peak hours unless you're actively eating or working.
- o Tip your server.

Gyms
- o Don't camp on machines. Rotate after sets.
- o Wipe down gear. Re-rack your weights.
- o No scrolling mid-set while people wait.

Parking Lots
- o Park straight. Inside the lines. One motion.
- o Don't hover behind someone walking to their car. Give them space.
- o Move briskly at curbs, elevators, and pedestrian crossings. These aren't lounge zones.

Movement & Etiquette ROI Table

Subtraction System	Hours Saved Yearly	Days Saved Lifetime	Annual Value	Lifetime Value
Escalator discipline	2.2	4.5	$108	$5,417
Doorway/hall blocking	4.3	9	$217	$10,833
Crosswalk awareness	4.3	9	$217	$10,833
Trail efficiency	4.3	9	$217	$10,833
Cycling shortcut logic	4.3	9	$217	$10,833
Line-readiness	4.3	9	$217	$10,833
Noise & space etiquette	4.3	9	$217	$10,833

Strategic Architect Rule

Move with a purpose even if you don't have one.

Every blocked hallway, every slow scroll, every half-step stall is friction, on the system, and on your day. Mastering these systems will endear you to other, like-minded people.

This isn't about being in a hurry. It's about being aware of flow, friction, and space. Your environment is shared. Act like it.

SECTION IV: *Home Base*

A Well-Run House Is a Force Multiplier

Turn your house into a background system that supports you, without demanding your attention.

Fire-and-Forget Income

I built a fun diplomatic-themed clothing and office gear store in a weekend with ideas from a good friend and my wife. I had a Shopify storefront, a print-on-demand backend, and a handful of diplomacy-themed designs I'd already created. No inventory. No shipping. No fulfillment. I don't pay for anything until someone buys and when they do, the profit is automatic. It costs me $40 a month to run. That's it. No spreadsheets, no boxes in my garage, no "I'll get to it later." The system is simple: design once, upload, forget. Months go by where I don't touch it, and it still pays me. That's a Subtraction System. Not just saved time. Recurring bandwidth and cash.

Chapter 1: Chore Elimination

Tales From the Field – Buy Time. Not Just Clean Floors.

When we were stationed in India, household help was very inexpensive. When the baby came, we didn't even think about it. We hired a driver, a nanny, and a part-time housekeeper, freeing us to go to work and have time to spend with our new son. Being able to zonk out or work during the hour-long Mumbai commute (five kilometers—yes, traffic was that bad) knowing our son was taken care of and that dinner would be on the table in a clean house, was more than worth the expense.

A 2017 Harvard study found that people who bought time by outsourcing drudgery were significantly happier. [9] Time is not just money. It is also satisfaction.

Core Problem

Vacuuming isn't noble. Folding laundry isn't a rite of passage. These are low-return tasks that automation and batching can handle better.

You're not too good to do chores, but your time is too valuable to do them inefficiently.

Systems / Tactics

Robot Vacuum
- Create a "safe zone" (cord control, open layout) and schedule it to run daily or while you're out.
- You never "vacuum the floor"; you just empty the robot.

Batch Laundry
- Wash once per week. Fold once per week.
- Daily loads are for people trying to feel busy.

---

[9] A. V. Whillans et al., "Buying Time Promotes Happiness," *Proceedings of the National Academy of Sciences of the United States of America* 114, no. 32 (2017): 8523–8527.

No-Fold Zone
- Socks and underwear go straight from the basket to the drawer (I only wear Balega No-Show Merino Blister Resist socks and Tracksmith Merino boxer briefs).
- If you're folding underwear, you've lost the plot.

Grocery Pickup or Delivery
- Order online, pick up curbside in five minutes, or schedule delivery.
- In-store browsing = 45 minutes of unpaid product handling. If delivery saves you 40 minutes and costs under 67% of your hourly rate, do the math.

Subscriptions for Essentials
- Use auto-delivery or subscribe-and-save from online retailers with free shipping for household staples (detergent, soap, toothpaste).
- If you're still manually shopping for paper towels and toilet paper, figure out your quarterly need and automate it.

Chore ROI Table

Subtraction System	Minutes Saved Daily	Hours Saved Yearly	Days Saved Lifetime	Annual Value	Lifetime Value
Robot vacuum	8.6	52.3	109	$2,615	$130,750
Grocery pickup/delivery	4.3	26.2	54.5	$1,310	$65,396
Batch laundry (vs. daily)	2.1	12.8	26.7	$639	$31,938
No-fold policy (socks/underwear)	2	12.2	25.4	$608	$30,417

Sacred Cow That Needs Killing: You Don't Need to Separate by Color

The idea that you need to separate whites, darks, and colors comes from the 1960s, when dyes bled, fabrics were unprocessed, and washers were basically blunt instruments. Obviously, there are some cases where you might not want to risk it; use your best judgement, Strategic Architect.

Modern reality:
- Cold water + modern detergent = no bleed.
- Most clothes are colorfast unless brand new.
- You're not washing raw denim or red wool sweaters on hot.

If it's not brand new or vintage, throw it all in together. Wash cold. Use a detergent with color guard. Done.

Time ROI – Skip Color Sorting

Subtraction System	Minutes Saved Daily	Hours Saved Yearly	Days Saved Lifetime	Annual Value	Lifetime Value
Eliminating color separation in laundry	1.4	8.5	17.7	$426	$21,292

Chapter 2: Appliances: Let the Machines Do the Work

Tales From the Field – Stop Babysitting the Machines

Appliances should be teammates, not time sinks. But too often, they become maintenance nightmares that require more human effort than they're worth.

I told this story at the beginning of the book, but as my "Seminal Moment," it bears repeating.

As a kid, I hated emptying the dehumidifier with the burning intensity of a thousand suns. Lift. Dump. Replace. Repeat. It was mindless, inefficient, and worst of all: avoidable.

Years later, stationed in Port of Spain, I finally solved it. I elevated the unit, ran a hose to a drain, and let gravity do the work. That four-minute fix permanently killed a task that had annoyed me for two decades.

Core Problem – The Dehumidifier Doctrine

If a device needs daily human input to do its job, it's a bad system. Period.

Appliances aren't upgrades unless they buy back time. People brag about their hardware, but they're still doing much of the work themselves.

Systems / Tactics – Appliance Upgrades That Pay for Themselves

Coffee Makers
- **Problem:** Daily setup, cleanup, and variable quality
- **Fix:** Use a programmable coffee maker with built-in grinder or pod system

Dishwashers
- **Problem:** Pre-scrubbing; inefficient cycles

- **Fix:** Use rinse-free pods and upgrade to a quiet, energy-efficient model, don't buy non-dishwasher/microwave safe items unless you absolutely have to. No fine China either, this isn't 1950.

Washing Machines & Dryers
- **Problem:** Forgotten loads, re-washing, endless folding
- **Fixes:**
  - Use delayed start or app-connected units
  - Hang dry apparel that can't withstand dryer (skip folding)
  - Mesh bags for socks/delicates
  - Pre-sort hampers (if you are going to do more than one load of laundry, then do a load per person, eliminating sorting clothes by family member)

Air Fryers / Instant Pots / Sous Vides
- **Problem:** Cooking takes too long and generates too much dirty cookware
- **Fix:** Use devices that consolidate prep, cook unattended, and reduce cleanup

Appliance ROI Table – Time & Value Recaptured

Subtraction System	Minutes Saved Daily	Hours Saved Yearly	Days Saved Lifetime	Annual Value	Lifetime Value
Coffee maker	2.1	12.8	26.6	$639	$31,938
Dishwasher	4	24.3	50.7	$1,217	$60,833
Washer/dryer	3	18.3	38	$913	$45,625
Smart cookers (air fryer, etc.)	5	30.4	63.4	$1,521	$76,042

Pro Tip: Never buy a tool that requires your constant presence to function. That's not help; it's delegation theater. Appliances should replace labor, not shift it.

Strategic Architect Rule
If it runs on power but depends on *you*, it's not automation, it's overhead. Buy once. Set up properly. Walk away.

Chapter 3: Shopping & Errands

Tales From the Field – Stop Shopping Like It's a Hobby

When I lived in DC, I knew someone who went to Target "just to browse" every Saturday.

That same person constantly said they didn't have time to read, work out, or cook, which was true, because they spent that time wandering down six aisles looking for a $40 dopamine hit and a throw pillow they didn't need.

That's not shopping. That's *procrastination*—and a *failure of prioritization*—disguised as productivity.

Core Problem – Errands Aren't Neutral

Errands either *buy you time* or *bleed it*.

Too many people shop reactively. One trip for toothpaste. Another for dog food. A quick stop that eats an hour. A forgotten item that becomes two trips.

That's not efficiency. That's self-inflicted overhead.

We discussed automating purchases earlier. Thus, the below is for stuff you either cannot (or refuse to) automate.

Systems / Tactics

1. **Maintain a Shared Household List**
   o One cloud-based list (e.g. Google Keep), updated in real time. The entire household uses it.
   o No duplicate trips. No forgotten items.
2. **Batch Errands Weekly**
   o One loop per week. Map your route. Stack stops logically.
   o Treat errands like a mission, not a vibe.

3. **Buy in Bulk** (Strategically)
   o You probably don't need a bunker of canned goods (but you can have it if you want).
   o But for items you use constantly (e.g. toilet paper, soap, rice, oats, nuts, protein powder), bulk saves trips, money, and brainpower.

Repeat Purchases & Replenishment

Every re-buy is a stress loop. Close them.
- Bulk order quarterly, not weekly.
- Build a Gift List:
   o Birthdays
   o Anniversaries
   o Major holidays
   o Pre-select gifts or gestures
   o Add reminders to your calendar noting gift ideas and status where appropriate

Shopping & Errand ROI Table

Subtraction System	Minutes Saved Daily	Hours Saved Yearly	Days Saved Lifetime	Annual Value	Lifetime Value
Batching errands	4	24.3	50.7	$1,217	$60,833
Shared household list	1	6.1	12.7	$304	$15,208

Chapter 4: Domestic Systems Architecture

Tales From the Field – If Your Family Runs on Vibes, Your Bandwidth Dies

Logistics doesn't stop at the embassy gate or the ops floor. A home without systems is just a slow-motion collapse with groceries.

What saves time, reduces arguments, and keeps everyone moving? Clarity. Rhythm. Assigned roles. Your home should run as well as your best squad.

Core Problem

Most homes don't need more togetherness. They need less confusion.

If everything depends on memory, goodwill, or last-minute hustle, you're already losing. *Systems don't kill spontaneity. They protect it.*

Systems / Tactics – Bandwidth Reclamation That Wins the Week

Shared Calendar = Shared Reality
- Use Google Calendar, Cozi, or Outlook
- Color-code by person
- Include events, school closures, travel, birthdays, bills
- No more "I didn't know."

The Sunday Sync (15 Minutes, Every Week)
- Review the shared calendar
- Determine logistics (events, pickups, travel)
- Assign roles
- Confirm kit status, per below
- Everyone hears it. Everyone knows their lane.

Pre-Packed Kits Every high-friction activity gets its own **go bag**:

- School backpacks, work briefcases
- Sports gear
- Overnight kit for kids (just in case)
- Travel kit

Restock as needed. Grab and go.

Default Meals = Fewer Decisions

You're not running a restaurant. You're running a base camp.
- Monday: pasta
- Tuesday: tacos
- Wednesday: leftovers
- Thursday: rice bowls
- Friday: freezer night

Repeat until morale improves.

Task Delegation = Early Leadership

If your kid can work an iPad, they can run the dishwasher.
- Assign small chores
- Rotate responsibilities weekly
- Reward consistency, not perfection

Chore Outsourcing (use when ROI-positive, but many are cost-prohibitive)
- Housecleaning (biweekly or monthly)
- Laundry service (expensive; probably better to just do it yourself)
- Lawn care (minimize areas requiring weed whacking)
- Leaf and snow removal (my pick: set-and-forget plow service)

If you make $50/hour and spend two hours scrubbing grout, **you're losing money.**

Family Logistics ROI Table

Subtraction System	Minutes Saved Daily	Hours Saved Yearly	Days Saved Lifetime	Annual Value	Lifetime Value
Calendar + Sunday Sync	5	30.4	63.4	$1,521	$76,042
Pre-packed kits	3.5	21.3	44.4	$1,065	$53,229
Default meal system	4.6	28.0	58.3	$1,399	$69,958
Delegated chores	9.2	56.0	116.6	$2,798	$139,917
Outsourced chores	5	30.4	63.4	$1,521	$76,042

Strategic Insight

When every person in your household operates on systems, the bandwidth multiplies.

One synced calendar, one chore schedule, one kit strategy, run across four people for 50 years, returns more than 7,000 hours and $360,000 in reclaimed value.

Childcare & School Logistics
Stability = bandwidth. Predictability = peace.
- Backpack packed the night before
- Homework station always stocked
- Three-bin paper system: urgent, action, archive
- Use shared digital calendar to sync school events

Social Life & Obligations
Saying "no" isn't rude. It's responsible.
- Pre-block "yes" time: travel, friend hangs, events
- Build templates for RSVPs, condolences, follow-ups
- Keep a "people I care about" list. Review quarterly.

Total Potential Gain
These aren't minor upgrades. These are *compound systems stacked across your life*.
- **Time saved:** 150–200 hours/year
- **Value reclaimed:** $7,500–$10,000+
- **Cognitive friction removed:** priceless

Strategic Architect Rule
A home with rhythm survives chaos.

There's a reason why military units establish a battle rhythm during prolonged operations. A battle rhythm is just your regular routine—how your day, week, or month runs by default. It's the appointments you always have, the homework you always do, the check-ins that show up like clockwork. Every team, family, unit, and company has a battle rhythm, even if they don't call it that.

A good battle rhythm keeps everyone in sync and focused. A bad one slowly drowns you in recurring junk.

People must realize they're not overwhelmed because they're bad at time management. They're overwhelmed because they've inherited a bloated, undisciplined rhythm, and never stopped to fix it.

This book gives you the tools to do exactly that: to audit your rhythm, kill the clutter, and build a cadence that works for your brain, your bandwidth, and your mission.

The fewer decisions you make under stress, the stronger your system is.

Don't just live in your household; operate it. Like it matters. Because it does.

Chapter 5: Paying Bills – Build It Once, Never Touch It Again

Core Problem

Paying bills isn't just a chore. It's a friction loop, and most people get caught in it every week.

Every login. Every "forgot password." Every "I'll do it later." It all adds up: lost time, late fees, mental clutter.

If your bill pay system still needs your presence, it's not a system.

Systems / Tactics – One-Time Setups That Free You Forever

Automate Every Bill That Won't Bankrupt You.
Set up auto-pay for:
- Mortgage / rent
- Credit cards (pay **full balance**)
- Utilities (gas, electric, water, trash)
- Insurance (auto, home, health, life)
- Cell + internet
- Subscriptions (cable, streaming, magazines, apps, etc.)
- Savings
- Investments

Take Advantage of Alerts
- Set bank alerts for any transactions over $500. You'll still catch most anomalies without logging in daily. Use in-app alerts, not email. Less spam, faster signal.

Use a Dedicated Bill-Pay Account
Route all recurring payments through one credit card or checking account.
- Separates ops from flex spend
- Simplifies audits
- Limits fraud exposure

- Creates a clean ledger for tax prep or disputes

Go Fully Digital
- Opt in to eStatements
- Route all billing emails into one smart folder
- Save PDFs of critical items to a cloud folder (Google Drive, Dropbox, etc.)
- Use dashboards (e.g. Mint, YNAB, Monarch)

Quarterly Financial Review/Checkpoint
Set a 30-minute block as a recurring calendar event every three months to analyze your financial landscape for:
- Rate hikes? Renegotiate.
- Ghost subscriptions? Cancel.
- Unnecessary services? Trim fat.
- Insurance scope? Still fit your risk profile?
- Anomalous transactions? Contest them.
- Insurance
- Open enrollment
- Subscription review
- Credit monitoring

ROI Table – Managing Finances the Lazy Way

Subtraction System	Minutes Saved Daily	Hours Saved Yearly	Days Saved Lifetime	Annual Value	Lifetime Value
Manual bill pay eliminated	3	18.3	38	$913	$45,625
Late fees / overdrafts avoided	0	0	0	$100	$5,000
Audit savings	0	0	0	$300	$15,000

Strategic Architect Rule
If you touch it more than once, it's broken.

Bills should run silently in the background. You only surface to audit, cancel, or correct.

Build the system once. Reap the bandwidth forever

Chapter 6: Bandwidth for Aging Parents - Support Without Losing Yourself

Tales From the Field – Don't Wait Until the Crisis

Supporting aging parents is inevitable. Doing it reactively is optional.

I've seen what happens when the system isn't in place: One ER visit triggers hours of paperwork, conflicting updates, and emotional whiplash. No one knows the meds. No one knows the wishes. Everyone panics.

A system won't fix aging. But it will keep you from drowning in it.

Core Problem

Most people build nothing until everything breaks.

And once you're in crisis mode, tracking down ID cards, asking about prescriptions, calling six providers. You're already burned out.

Bandwidth in elder care doesn't mean *control*. It means *structure*.

Systems / Tactics – Family Support Structures

Medical Folder (Digital + Physical)
Keep it simple. Update quarterly or as needed.
- Full medication list with dosages and timing
- Names, specialties, and contacts for all providers
- Insurance card scans and policy summaries
- Copy of driver's license, Medicare card, state ID
- Summary of major conditions, allergies, surgeries

Store in two places:
- Cloud folder (e.g. Google Drive, Dropbox)
- Printed binder in a known location

Shared Legal Folder (Digital + Physical)
Accessible to the people who need it; no scavenger hunt required.
- Power of attorney (medical and financial)
- Will
- Advance directive
- End-of-life preferences
- Emergency contact list (doctors, lawyer, financial advisor, executor)

Store in two places:
- Cloud folder (e.g. Google Drive, Dropbox)
- Printed binder in a known location

Call Scripts + Text Templates
Don't rely on memory or mood.
- **Call script** to keep updates consistent:
  - "How's your sleep, appetite, energy?"
  - "Any new meds or appointments?"
  - "Need help refilling anything?"
- **Reusable text** for quick check-ins:
  - "Hi, anything new this week medically? Just want to stay current."

Dedicated Check-In Calendar Events
- 15-minute biweekly time block
- Use it for check-ins, scanning updates, or managing paperwork
- Adds rhythm. Reduces the sense of being "always behind"

ROI Table – Supporting Parents Without Losing Yourself (20-Year Lifetime Values)

Subtraction System	Minutes Saved Daily	Hours Saved Yearly	Days Saved Lifetime	Annual Value	Lifetime Value
Medical folder, Legal/doc storage, Standard scripts/templates, Scheduled check-ins, Coordination time avoided	5	30.5	63.5	$1,520	$30,415

Strategic Architect Rule
Supporting your parents shouldn't cost you your life. You're not being cold by creating structure. You're being kind, to them and to yourself.

Systems don't remove the burden. They **distribute** it. And they keep it from breaking you when the phone rings.

Chapter 7: Hidden Calories – The Slow Bloat You Don't Notice

The Hard Math First

If you want to lose weight, the most effective method (still, always) is counting calories.

Not guessing. Not vibes. Counting. Because your body runs on physics, not motivation.

This entire book is about using math to reclaim time, money, and energy. Calorie tracking is the same tool applied to your fuel economy. You're not "dieting"; you're identifying invisible inputs and mitigating them.

The average American gains 1–2 pounds per year without realizing it.[10] That's not failure. That's untracked inputs in a closed system.

So, let's do what we do best: find the invisible inefficiencies, put a number on them, and build a better system.

Tales From the Field – The Coke That Got Me

I once did the math on the 12 oz Cherry Coke I drank every day. That one bottle was 150 calories. That means I was unknowingly consuming the equivalent of *a third of a meal*—just from sugar water. Over a year, that's 55,000 calories. Not food. Not protein. Not anything that made me full. Just the delivery vehicle for a habit I didn't question. I wasn't gaining weight because of laziness or gluttony. I was gaining it because I was consuming excess calories from invisible places, every single day. I finally got an app to count calories to tell me just how many I was consuming each day. It was a lot. But rather than keep paying for the app subscription, I learned how to mentally tally up my macros and calories, ditched the app ($20 a month savings), and reaped a 20-pound weight reduction in six months. And I've kept it off. I still love Cherry Coke; I just drink it less.

---

[10]Harvard T.H. Chan School of Public Health. "Healthy Weight." Nutrition Source. Accessed June 12, 2025.

Core Problem

People don't gain weight from the occasional dessert binges or cheat meals. They gain it from default settings: the bread, the sugar, the butter, the dressing, the fast food, the soda, the fourth beer.

The human body doesn't track calories intuitively. You don't "feel" 270 extra calories from Cherry Coke. But your body absorbs them and stores them for later.

Systems / Tactics – Invisible Cuts That Add Up

Limit Soda Intake to No More Than One a Day
- ~150 calories per can
- That's 54,750 calories per year
- Equivalent of 15.6 pounds of fat

Cut Back on the Sugary Coffee
- Grande vanilla latte: ~250 calories
- Same daily math = 91,250/year → 26 pounds
- Instead, brew black and add 2 tablespoons frothed milk or your favorite non-dairy alternative, a fraction of the calories at a fraction of the price

Rethink Those Two Slices of White Bread
- ~200 calories from an empty carb with no fiber
- Sub in lettuce wraps, thin-sliced varieties, half-sandwich, or skip it altogether
- Alternatively, opt for whole grain breads; although they don't save on calories, they'll better satiate you, thanks to their higher fiber content.

Swap Salad Dressings
- Ranch or Caesar: 2 tablespoons = ~130–150 calories
- Double it (which most people do) = 260–300 calories on a "healthy" salad
- Use "light" versions, measure, or switch to lemon juice + herbs

Choose Grilled Instead of Fried
- Fried chicken sandwich = 500–600 calories
- Grilled version = ~350
- Same protein. Less fat, less regret.

Be Cognizant of Mayonnaise / Butter / "Small Adds"
- Mayo: 1 tablespoon = 90 calories
- Butter on toast, oil drizzle on pasta, extra cheese: all in the 50–150 calorie range
- You do these every day; you just don't notice.

Invisible Calorie ROI Table (3,500 Calories = 1 Pound of Fat)

Habit	Daily Calories	Yearly Calories	Yearly Pounds	Lifetime Calories	Lifetime Pounds
One soda	150	54,750	15.6	2,737,500	780
One sugary latte	250	91,250	26	4,562,500	1,300
Two slices of sandwich bread	200	73,000	21	3,650,000	1,040
Salad w/4 tbsp ranch	300	109,500	31	5,475,000	1,560
Mayo on sandwich (1 tbsp)	90	32,850	9.4	1,642,500	468
Fried instead of grilled	200	73,000	21	3,650,000	1,040

The extras add up, especially in terms of yearly and lifetime totals.

Strategic Architect Rule
You don't have to starve. You just have to be mindful.

Calories hide in the places you've stopped paying attention to. Build systems that default to clean inputs, visible quantities, and easy substitutes. Willpower fades. **Design doesn't.**

SECTION V: *Subtract to Learn*

Cut the Noise; Keep What Matters

Build a system that's low-effort, high-retention, and runs quietly in the background.

Thinking at 180 Beats Per Minute

A million years ago in Iraq, just after getting blown up (again) by a roadside bomb, I found myself calculating.

Not emotionally. Not metaphorically. I was running numbers in my head while my heart thudded at 180 beats per minute.

Distance. Direction. Disposition. Where are our friendlies? Do I have time to maneuver (maneuver? Go where? lol). What's our next move? Is this a complex attack or a one-off? Who's wounded? Anyone? Am I? Did I radio for help? Do I need to?

I didn't realize it then, but I had trained for this. Not at the Infantry School at Fort Benning, but years earlier, when I taught myself to speak backwards for fun. When I did mental math while running long distances. When I tried to keep my mind calm while my body redlined.

I wasn't just building cognitive endurance. I was teaching my brain to make decisions under duress and pressure.

That's the point of subtracting input noise. Every unnecessary notification, every slow-loading webpage, every loud opinion on your feed steals your margin for real cognition.

Bandwidth is more than time. It's clarity under fire. And when things break, it's the only thing that matters.

Chapter 1: Learning Bandwidth

Tales From the Field – Learning Can Be Passive, Portable, and Compounding

I don't "make time" for learning. I integrate it. Every run, every commute, every walk to the store is an opportunity to sharpen the blade. The goal isn't effort; it's integration.

Core Problem

If you're only learning when you sit down to study, you're moving too slowly.

We live in a golden age of signal, books, lectures, interviews, analysis, and *most of it goes unused because there's no system.*

Systems / Tactics – The Learning Operating System

Smart Audio Strategy
- Podcasts at 1.25x–1.5x speed (1.25x is my default)
- Use apps with speed presets and silence skip, such as Overcast or Spotify
- Auto-download new episodes from trusted shows
- Use premium or skip settings to block ads
- Consider pairing topic to intensity:
    - Runs → light, conversational
    - Drives → heavy, dense, strategic
    - Walks → philosophical

Learning Operating System Setup
- Use a note-taking app like Readwise to pull highlights from:
    - Digital e-readers (e.g. Kindle)
    - Social media
    - PDFs
    - Web articles

- Feed highlights into a system such as Notion's "Brain Vault" or even just use the Notes app on your phone
  - Review weekly (can use Sunday Sync block)
  - Tag by topic, actionability, or cross-domain pattern
- Rotate fiction and non-fiction
  - Fiction = pattern recognition + creativity
  - Non-fiction = models, tools, frameworks

Learning ROI Table

Subtraction System	Minutes Saved Daily	Hours Saved Yearly	Days Saved Lifetime	Annual Value	Lifetime Value
Passive learning (podcasts/audio)	10	43.3	90.3	$2,167	$108,333
Speed + ad skip + pairing logic	5.8	25.1	52.4	$1,257	$62,833
Readwise → Notion review loop	5.8	25.1	52.4	$1,257	$62,833

Strategic Architect Rule

Don't try to learn harder. Build a system that learns for you. Turn the background into brain gain. If you move, you learn. If you eat, you listen. If you highlight, you review.

That's not hustle (we reject hustle culture here). That's compounding cognition.

Chapter 2: Influence Bandwidth – Writing, Speaking, Leading

Tales From the Field – I Didn't Study for College. I Studied for the Mission.

The best communicators don't wing it (but it often looks like they do). They systemize clarity the same way they'd plan a raid, prep for a deployment, or write a negotiation brief.

I never studied in high school. Didn't study in college. Skated through grad school.

But I studied for the Foreign Service Oral Assessment (FSOA) like my career depended on it, because it did. The stakes were simply higher and I adapted to them.

I am terrible at job interviews. I am not unaware of this irony, given that I interview at least a dozen times every two to three years for a new job. Interviews just aren't my thing. But for the FSOA, which includes a one-hour structured interview, I prepped. To do so, I memorized seven true, autobiographical vignettes: tight, easy stories that mapped directly onto the 13 Dimensions by which a Foreign Service Officer Candidate is evaluated. Each vignette was a flexible tool that covered multiple Dimensions, meaning I could use many of them no matter which questions were asked. A single vignette could answer three questions. Under stress, that mattered.

When the interview began—one hour, no notes, no second chances—I wasn't grasping.

That wasn't just charisma (remember charisma ≠ leadership; charisma = theater). That was preparation as a weapon.

If you're sharpening your message during the delivery, you're already behind.

Core Problem

Too many high performers treat writing and speaking as spontaneous art.
That's fine, if you are ok with inconsistent results. But if you want to be clear and eloquent, having some off-the-shelf pieces that really work is a great time saver.

Influence is a system. Templates (not just for spoken bits, elevator pitches, or interviews but for more mundane uses as well) save time, but more importantly, they preserve *clarity under pressure*.

Systems / Tactics – Influence That Scales

Template Arsenal
- **Thank-you notes** (post-meeting, gift, milestone)
- **LinkedIn introductions** (warm "no thank you" / hard-close recruiting)
- **Public speaking openings** (10-second attention hook + context)
- **Weekly briefs** (internal updates, external partner touchpoints)
- **Executive summaries** (one-pager format: problem, solution, ask, risk)

Leadership Reuse Systems
- **Swipe file of strong writing**
  - Save standout phrases from employee evaluations, op-eds, cover letters, bios
  - Pull from other people as well; annotate and tag for fast repurposing
- **30-second origin story**
  - Built for intros, panels, and chance encounters
  - Two versions: career arc and current mission
  - Memorize the first line. Improvise the rest.
- **Slide & proposal templates**
  - Save slide deck shells for pitches, updates
  - Use pre-built layouts for flow and speed
  - Store in your cloud drive, labeled for reuse

ROI Table – Influence Systems

Subtraction System	Minutes Saved Daily	Hours Saved Yearly	Days Saved Lifetime	Annual Value	Lifetime Value
Templates for writing/speaking	4.6	19.9	41.5	$997	$49,833
Swipe file + reuse	1.2	5.2	10.8	$260	$13,000
Prebuilt slide decks + one-pagers	2.3	10	20.8	$498	$24,917
Origin story & intro prep	0.5	2.2	4.5	$108	$5,417

Strategic Architect Rule
You don't get extra points for writing from scratch. *Influence compounds when you stop improvising and start operationalizing.*

Save the flair for the moment that needs it. Until then: template, store, and use. Your clarity deserves the system it needs.

Honestly, save every written product you create. Discipline by Subtraction was created from hundreds of smaller documents produced over the last thirty years. Many documents contained small bits of knowledge to write this book, which would have been lost if I just deleted them.

Sidebar: Make It Easy for Others to Help You

Jerry Maguire said it best to Rod Tidwell: "Help me help you."

When seeking assistance or support, providing clear, concise information can significantly increase the likelihood of a positive response.

Consider the following practices:

- Provide drafts or bullet points: If requesting a letter of recommendation or an evaluation, offer a draft or key points to guide the writer. This not only saves them time but also ensures that your achievements are accurately represented. And aim high—write like you're awesome and this becomes "the first number" of the "negotiation (because every human interaction is a negotiation of some sort) anchor point. See Section II Chapter 1: Negotiation Bandwidth – Winning Without Burning Bridges, for more info.

- Suggest courses of action: When proposing policy changes or new initiatives, present well-developed options that align with your preferred outcomes. This approach facilitates decision-making and demonstrates your proactive engagement.

- Understand the decision-making process: Recognize that often, staff members formulate policy options, and leaders choose from these. By contributing effectively to this process, you can influence outcomes even without holding a top position.

> "Power was not the province of those who made choices. Power was the ability to set the context in which choices were made."
> —Seth Dickinson, The Traitor Baru Cormorant

Author's Note: Dickinson's quote slaps so hard because it exposes the real hierarchy. Power doesn't come from choosing; it comes from controlling the menu. No president, no CEO, no dictator runs everything. They don't have the *bandwidth*. They necessarily rely on staff (analysts, chiefs of staff, advisors, deputies) to filter, frame options, and pick what gets seen.

There is no such thing as a "full menu" of choices. Every leader only sees the curated list. That list is the battlefield. The people who curate the list? They are the ones holding real power.

Chapter 3: Mind Games – Unusual Habits That Sharpen the Edge

Not everything needs to be practical; just effective.

Tales From the Field

As a kid, I taught myself to speak backwards. Not for school. Not for show. Just because I was bored and the words were right in front of me.

Years later, I realized it trained my brain to hear and manipulate phonemes in ways no spelling lessons could. It also turned out to be surprisingly useful for reading upside-down documents on the desks of bankers and bureaucrats in front of me.

In my twenties, I started doing mental math while running: long division, square roots, percentage calculations, as difficult as I could go. Elevated heart rate = simulated duress.

At the time, it was just a game. But now? I'm convinced it's why I can think calmly under pressure. I trained my brain and locked in those neural pathways to solve problems while my heart rate was redlining.

Because when your heart is at 180 bpm and the bullets are flying …

"If you can keep your head when all about you
    Are losing theirs and blaming it on you,
If you can trust yourself when all men doubt you,
    But make allowance for their doubting too…
…you'll be a Man, my son!"

— "If" by Rudyard Kipling (liberally excerpted)

In all seriousness: if you can slow your brain while everything else accelerates and then use that calm to direct your adrenaline-charged body, that's a superpower.

Core Problem

Cognitive performance advice is boring. Meditate. Journal. Eat fish.

Valid, I guess? But common.

In my experience, some of the best mental upgrades come from weird, low-cost habits that seem useless on the surface ... until they're not.

Systems / Tactics – Build a Bandwidth-Oriented Mind Gym

These are optional reps for your brain. Pick one. Do it when you have time. Let it compound.

Verbal Play
- Speak backwards
- Read or write upside down
- Translate common phrases into a foreign language in your head

ROI: Increases verbal agility, pattern recognition, and phonetic memory.

Cognitive Exercises Under Load
- Solve math problems while lifting or swimming
- Summarize complex ideas while holding a plank
- Try memory recall drills during light workouts

ROI: Trains executive function under physical stress.

Constraint Games
- Debate a topic from the opposite side
- Give 30-second explanations of complex issues with no "um" or "like"
- Use only one-syllable words to describe your job
- Complete crossword puzzles
- Gamify with language or logic apps such as Wordle, Spelling Bee, Connections

ROI: Builds mental discipline, creativity, and control.

Recall Challenges
- Mentally map your route from memory
- Reconstruct a conversation word for word
- Visualize your grocery list in spatial order

ROI: Improves working memory, attention, and focus endurance.

Strategic Architect Rule
If a game rewires your brain for performance, **it's not a waste of time.** Even if it looks ridiculous (I know it looks ridiculous, lol).

The ROI isn't just in what it trains; it's in how it unlocks frictionless skill acquisition everywhere else.

Closing Thought

This isn't hacking. It's building a new system.

Chapter 4: ROI-Based Scam Detection

If it looks real and benefits them, assume they invested effort, and treat it like a high-stakes threat.

Tales From the Field – The $10,000 Invoice Scam

I received an email from a vendor asking me to reprocess a payment. It looked real.
- Company name was right.
- Formatting was clean.
- Email tone was sharp and professional.
- They referenced invoice we'd already paid.

One search confirmed it: fake.

But this wasn't a spam blast or typo-filled cash grab. They'd done their homework: real names, real vendor history, real account numbers.

They weren't trying to steal $100. They wanted $10,000.

And they almost got it.

Core Problem – Scammers Follow ROI Logic (Scammers: they're just like us!)

Low-effort scams go wide, hoping for small wins. High-effort scams go narrow, targeting big payouts.

But most people still judge a scam merely by how it looks. You also need to judge it by how much effort they put into it.

If it's sloppy? It's a numbers game. If it's slick? It's a surgical extraction attempt.

Systems / Tactics – How to Read the ROI Behind the Scam

1. **Use the Effort-to-Extraction Ratio**
   Ask:

- o Did they use your name?
- o Did they match a real invoice or vendor name?
- o Does it look like they pulled your actual org chart or billing flow?

If yes, they're aiming for four or five figures.

Treat it like an active threat, not a curiosity.

2. **Slow Down the Decision Loop**

Urgency is their weapon. Delay is your armor.

Every extra step—searching past invoices, calling the vendor, asking a colleague—reduces their ROI and raises yours. Slow is secure.

3. **Know Your Friction Points**

If you don't know:

- o Who processes what
- o What real invoices look like
- o Who signs off on large payments

Then you'll be the weakest link.

If your system is opaque to you, it's wide open to them.

So, build a basic map of:

- o Vendor payment flows
- o Internal sign-off processes
- o Escalation points

ROI Table – Scam Effort vs. Payout Risk

Scam Type	Effort Level	Targeted Value	Detection Difficulty	Risk If Missed
Generic spam email	Low	<$100	Low	Low
Phishing login page	Medium	Account credentials	Medium	High (access risk)
Vendor invoice spoof	High	$1,000–$10,000+	High	Catastrophic
Executive impersonation	Very High	$10,000–$1M+	Very High	Catastrophic

Strategic Architect Rule

If it looks real and benefits them, assume it's targeted. And if it's targeted, they've done the ROI math.

So should you.

Scam defense isn't about paranoia, it's about pattern recognition. Read the play, slow the pace, and break their return on investment.

Seriously: slow everything down to a crawl if you suspect a scam. This time, the friction is worth it.

Chapter 5: The ROI of Deception – Spot Lies by Tracking Effort, Gain, and Bandwidth

Lies aren't mistakes, they're economic decisions. They're calculated investments—and they leave fingerprints.

Tales From the Field – The ROI Profile of a Lie

Some years back, I sat across from a man whose story didn't add up. He described a committed relationship, but couldn't recall basic shared experiences—no memories of favorite meals, vacations, or even which side of the bed his partner slept on.

It was supposed to be a straightforward conversation. But the longer we talked, the more intricate the lie became. He'd coordinated timelines, rehearsed anecdotes, even cross-checked his story against a fake school calendar to support the illusion.

It wasn't desperate. It was calculated. A deception designed for maximum return on investment. The more energy he poured into it, the more seams appeared—because every added layer increased friction and fragility.

We're not getting into facial tics or pulse rates here. This is field-ready deception detection. You know it's fake not because it's poorly built, but because it's overbuilt—and overbuilding has a cost.

Core Problem

Lies are rarely emotional. They're transactional.

They are rarely efficient. They must be remembered, rehearsed, and supported.

Whether it's a teenager, coworker, vendor, or world leader, the structure is the same: Effort vs. reward vs. risk.

Truth carries no overhead, you just say what really happened. Lies carry a bandwidth cost: mental, verbal, logistical. If you want to spot deception, don't play psychologist. Play investor.

Systems / Tactics – How to Detect Lies Without Guesswork

1. **Apply the Effort-Gain-Risk Model**
   Ask:
   o   How much does this person stand to gain?
   o   How much does it cost for them to lie?
   o   How risky is getting caught?
   High gain + low effort + low risk = high lie likelihood.
   Low gain + high risk? That's often when people stick to the truth, even if it hurts.

   Put more simply:

Factor	Question	What to Watch
Effort	Is this a simple or complex lie?	Long explanations, rehearsed stories
Gain	What's at stake if it works?	Jobs, money, reputation, freedom
Risk	What happens if they're caught?	Denial, shame, legal consequences

2. **Look for Friction in the Details**
   Lies require:
   o   Memory management
   o   Story synchronization
   o   Emotional alignment
   Thus, you must listen for:
   o   Corrections mid-sentence
   o   Vague timelines
   o   Irrelevant details that don't answer the question
   o   Perfect alignment with your expectations (which often means they're mirroring, not reporting)
   The truth is lumpy. The lie is clean, but over-polished.

3. **Watch for Over-Justification**
   If someone defends something before you challenge it, they're forecasting suspicion.
   Examples:
   o   "I would never do that …" (no one asked yet)
   o   "This is totally normal, I promise …" (why the disclaimer?)
   Truth doesn't usually come with a preemptive defense package.

4. **Map Motive to Bandwidth**
   Over-Polished Story: Too clean = too rehearsed
   Vague Timelines: No clear when/where = mental bandwidth leak
   Preemptive Defense: Denial before accusation = guilt prep
   Mirrored Emotion: Reads like what you wanted to hear

ROI Table – When Lies Leave Fingerprints

Signal	Effort	Risk If Caught	Payout Potential	Lie Likelihood
Vague timelines	Low	Low	Medium	Medium
Over-justification	Medium	Low	Medium	High
Polished, too-perfect story	High	Medium	High	High
Verifiable, high-risk claim	High	High	High	Low

Who's Lying and Why?

Each category has a signature risk/gain threshold.
Understand it, and you'll predict deception patterns.

Liar Type	Typical ROI Math
Employee	Avoids accountability, delays consequence, protects status
Teenager	Gains freedom, hides mistake, low cost if caught
Contractor/Vendor	Invoices up, liability down, hard to verify
Politician	Preserves image, narrative control, high tolerance window
Friend/Partner	Preserves relationship, avoids conflict, emotional shield

Strategic Architect Rule
Lies follow incentive curves.

Track (as mentioned above):
- How much does this person stand to gain?
- How much does it cost for them to lie?
- How risky is getting caught?

The truth doesn't need scaffolding. But every lie is a structure and structures leave blueprints.

If you can read ROI, you can discern a lie.

Coda: They Tell on Themselves

As a visa officer, I interviewed more than 35,000 people; thousands in Russian, and thousands in dozens of other languages using a translator. As a soldier, I've questioned hundreds, and I've interrogated dozens of high-value targets.

If there's one quiet throughline that holds across nearly all of them, including non-English speaking people, it's this:

People tend to tell on themselves. (If the American people had any idea how much of their national security was predicated on people telling on themselves, they'd be aghast.)

Sometimes it's accidental. Sometimes it's performative.

But often they'll give you the rope themselves, because they want you to see just how clever they were.

There's a universal human urge to feel smarter than the other guy, and a second urge to help someone out who seems confused. I lean into both in my interviews.

- "Sorry, I'm not sure I understand, can you walk me through how this works?"
- "Why is this lab closing? Budget shortfall?"
- "No one could have possibly been smart enough to concoct such an elaborate criminal enterprise, right?"

Framed innocently, questions like those don't trigger defenses. They open the door. Most people step through willingly, especially if they think you missed something.

And when someone doesn't give anything up? Ask more questions. From oblique angles, from the doors and corners.

Find the thread that feels off. The claim that doesn't square. Pull on it, gently, patiently.

Ask, "What would so-and-so say about this if I asked her?" to introduce the possibility that you have a witness with a contradicting statement. That statement doesn't even need to exist and neither does the witness, but the implication (that there may be a credible, contradicting account) will drive many liars closer to the truth. Just the threat of either changes the math.

Eventually, you'll land on a question they can't answer without lying. They'll try to maintain the story. But it's hard to keep a straight face when you've just told an objective mistruth out loud.

Even the seasoned ones blink. Their voice hitches. The pause gets just a little too long.

That's where the bandwidth is. Bandwidth isn't just what they reveal, it's what you listen for. Not in accusations. Not in confrontation. In simple questions.

Lie Detection Checklist
- Does this person stand to gain significantly? A little?
- Is the story too clean? (real life is messy)
- Are there signs of rehearsed emotion?
- What's missing that should be there?
- How easy would it be to verify?

Oblique Questions Sidebar
- "What would so-and-so say about this?"
- "I'm confused—can you explain again?"
- "Help me understand why this adds up…"

SECTION VI: *Life by Design*

Systems Do the Work, So You Can Live

Structure your remote setup, daily flow, and deep work blocks to eliminate noise, preserve energy, and take full control of your day.

One Template to Rule Them All

In a previous job , I found myself repeatedly decoding government policy cables—briefs intended to guide international engagement. Each time one came in, I had to search through blocks of text to answer the same basic questions: Who needs to act? What's the deadline? Can this document be shared? What are the follow-up requirements?

That metadata was there, somewhere, but never in the same place twice. Multiply that by five cables a week, across hundreds of posts, and you've got a global scavenger hunt for operational clarity.

So I built a fix. I mocked up a universal template that frontloaded the critical information in a predictable, top-level format—no bureaucratic turf battles, just design logic. I passed it along to HQ through informal channels. A few months later, HQ adopted about half of my recommendations.

The savings were real:
- Five cables per week × eight minutes saved per cable
- Across 280 posts and 52 weeks
- Equals over 9,700 hours annually—roughly 4.6 full-time positions
- At $150/hour fully loaded cost, that's $1.45 million in recaptured bandwidth

This is what subtraction architecture looks like. It's not about flash or authority. It's about structure that scales—small changes with systemic impact.

That's not optimization. That's architecture. When you create something that works once and then works everywhere, you're not just productive—you're a force multiplier.

Subtraction at this level doesn't live in checklists or inbox hacks. It lives in design decisions that compound. And this one was free.

Chapter 1: Million-Dollar Bandwidth – The Jammock® Case Study

I didn't build a million-dollar business to hustle. I built a system so I could disappear from it.

This chapter is the definitive case study in Strategic Laziness. How do you make a million dollars from your basement, while keeping your day job, avoiding hiring staff, and skipping hustle-culture pitfalls? You design the system once, then get out of its way.

The Origin

It started with a Jeep, a run, and no place to sit.

In 2005, I was a young Army infantry officer stationed at Fort Benning. I bought a Jeep Wrangler, and after runs off-post, I wanted somewhere to sit and relax. So, I rigged a hammock across the roll bars. Later, I built a custom version from trampoline material, wide enough to lie across, light enough to store, and durable enough to survive.

I called it the Jammock. Then I sat on the idea for seven years.

The Basement Lab

In 2012, I turned my basement into a workshop. Hot knives + trampoline fabric + sewing machine = DIY product R&D. I then installed the prototype Jammock on my Jeep and hosted a party at which I asked every guest to climb up and fill out a survey: comfort, price point, value, potential use cases. Afterwards, guests grabbed a beer and mingled. It worked: I got free product testing, brutally honest (in vino veritas) feedback, and a house full of my friends.

When I was ready, I contracted a U.S. manufacturer (Jeep owners want American-made). First production run: 100 tan units.
- Mistake: Most buyers apparently wanted black, and my brown Jammocks weren't selling (I sold 11 the first year).
- Lesson: Never assume what the market wants. Confirm it.

I was ready to fold. But my wife suggested a presale for the black version: get people to pay up front, validate demand, and fund production. On the first day, we sold 20 units. That paid for the entire run, and she saved the company.

Strategic Laziness Principle: Work hard once to never have to work hard again.

The System Design (I designed it to run without me)
- Set up a Shopify storefront with automated payments
- Integrated fulfillment through a U.S.-based 3PL warehouse
- Outsourced manufacturing to reduce cost
- Hired freelancers (Upwork) for branding, IP filings, and patent support
- Contracted a social media pro for marketing
- Filed a patent (slow, painful, worth it)
- Used a single credit card for all business expenses

Key Tools
- **Shopify** – Storefront + payment automation
- **3PL Warehouse** – Fulfillment without touching inventory
- **Upwork** – On-demand experts for design, legal, and IP
- **Contract Manufacturer** – Lower costs at scale
- **CPA** – Tax strategy + audit defense
- **One Credit Card** – Simplified tracking and rewards

Result? Jammock became a six-figure business. Best year: 3,000+ units at $100 a unit. All while I kept my day job.

There are a few key aspects I still handle, such as:
- Inventory monitoring
- Reorders
- Vendor payments (some still mail checks)
- IRS compliance (including surviving a three-year audit)

But day-to-day? The business runs itself. Time spent: One hour per week.

That's not hyperbole. At this point, I spend less time on Jammock per week than most people spend emptying dehumidifiers and folding socks. I built the thing once. I fixed the early breakpoints. I automated what mattered. Then I (mostly) left it alone.

Mistakes Were Made…
- DIY patent filing before paying a pro cost me seven years and $7K
- Early production error from failing to validate color demand
- Overpaid for a web developer early on (could've done it in an hour)
- Got behind on accounting and almost lost an IRS audit

The Audit
The IRS audited me over the course of 18 months for three tax years, claiming I owed $110K. I eventually won and they owed me $4K. But it only worked because I had:

- Faithfully used a separate business credit card for every purchase (thus, if I lost receipts, I had backups)
- Saved receipts and tracked sales (via Google Sheets)
- Hired a real accountant by the time it mattered
- Didn't cheat on my taxes (a key factor, as it turned out)

The audit nearly broke me, but the system proved defensible.

Why Jammock Worked

It wasn't a billion-dollar rocket ship. It didn't need to be. Jammock worked because it was small, sharp, and ruthlessly subtractive. I didn't follow startup gospel; I actually ignored most of it. I didn't scale first. I didn't chase growth. I built something useful, tested it with real money, and kept my overhead near zero. What follows is what I did and just as importantly, what I did not do.

What I Did:
- I built for the niche first and the broader market could wait
- I built it lean
- I outsourced everything non-core
- I validated every run with real dollars
- I automated before scaling

What I Didn't Do:
- I didn't hire permanent staff
- I didn't build a warehouse
- I didn't raise venture capital money
- I didn't spend every night on it
- I delegated. I pre-sold. I stayed lazy on purpose.

Chapter 2: Work From Home – The Bandwidth Superpower

Butts in seats is not a strategy.

Tales From the Field – COVID, Control, and a 90-Minute Reallocation

When COVID hit, I was a new father with a sustained workload, a toddler at home, and-suddenly-no commute, no dress code, and no office performance theater.

We were living in a tiny apartment in Northern Virginia. My suits stayed in the closet. My car stayed parked. And for the first time in years, I had something I hadn't accounted for: discretionary time.

Though my role still required high-focus work, we rotated in-office coverage, and much of my workload hit a strange holding pattern. There wasn't always a clear substitute for the usual meetings or secure workflows, which meant my schedule quietly thinned out. On most days:
- That commute? Gone.
- Lunch logistics? Gone.
- Putting on the D.C. armor every morning? Gone.

By the end of 2020, I was more productive, less reactive, and despite the chaos around me, mentally sharper than I'd been in years.

It wasn't magic. It was bandwidth, reallocated.

Core Problem

Work from home isn't a perk. It's an asymmetric strategic advantage—and most organizations are squandering it.

The average white-collar worker spends nearly an hour a day commuting. That's 240 hours a year of unrecoverable opportunity cost. Add wardrobe logistics, meal prep, decompression, and office noise—and you're looking at a daily tax on clarity and output.

Reversing that is not a lifestyle preference. It's an operational upgrade. The question isn't whether working from home gives you time. The question is: What are you doing with it?

Systems / Tactics – Make It Work Like It Matters

1. **Lock in the Commute Dividend**
   Don't just delete your commute. Reassign it.
   o **Morning zone:** podcasts, language lessons, idea incubation, deep thinking
   o **Evening zone:** walk, stretch, decompress deliberately
   55 minutes/day × 5 days/week = 4.6 hours/week
   That's 40 books a year. Or 300 workouts. Or a side project launched.
2. **Preset Your Launch Conditions**
   o **Auto-brew your coffee** (I know, we've talked about this before).
   o Set it for the same time every day. If you don't get up, it gets cold. That's a time-based forcing function.
   Default Zoom uniform.
   o One neutral background. One solid shirt. Pre-tied necktie and suit jacket nearby in case you need them. Sweatpants optional. No decisions needed.
   One work location.
   o Doesn't need to be fancy, but it needs to be defined.
   o Kitchen counter ≠ office.
   o Reclaim physical separation to enforce mental clarity.
3. **Hard Shutdown Ritual**
   o Close the laptop.
   o Kill Slack.
   o Exit the "office" space.
   o Signal to your brain: we're done.
   If you don't shut down, you're always "on," which means you're never fully rested, present, or clear.

Timeblock Like You Mean It

Time*	Focus
8:00–9:30	Deep work only
9:30–10:00	Email, Slack, low-friction comms
12:00–12:30	Lunch, walk, workout, or rest
3:00–4:00	Second deep work block
4:30 sharp	Shut it down

Time between blocks is for the other stuff that comes up during the workday

You don't work better because you're at home. You work better because you're finally allowed to control the throughput.

Sidebar: The Untapped ROI

For Employees:
Work from home erases the single largest tax on time—commuting—while eliminating smaller costs like gas, wardrobe, meals, and childcare logistics. What's left? Bandwidth. Mental clarity. The chance to run the day instead of reacting to it.

For Employers:
A 10-person remote team saves over $74K/year in hard costs alone, before factoring in retention, morale, or productivity gains. It's not just cheaper. It's stronger.

ROI Table – Employee-Side: Annual and Lifetime Value

Subtraction System	Minutes Saved Daily	Hours Saved Yearly	Days Saved Lifetime	Annual Value	Lifetime Value
Commute eliminated	55	238	496	$11,917	$595,833
Logistics prep	5	21.7	45.1	$1,083	$54,167
Meals + coffee	10	43.3	90.3	$2,167	$108,333
Appearance/wardrobe management	5	21.7	45.1	$1,083	$54,167
Decompression/re-ramp time	10	43.3	90.3	$2,167	$108,333
Childcare logistics buffer (10-year cap)	11.5	49.8	20.8	$498	$24,917

Employer-Side ROI – Small Business (10 Employees)

Cost Area	Annual In-Office Cost	Annual Work From Home Cost	Annual Savings
Commercial rent (1,500–2,000 sq ft @ $30/sq ft)	$45,000	$0	$45,000
Utilities + internet	$10,000	$0	$10,000
Office upkeep, maintenance & janitorial	$6,000	$0	$6,000
Furniture + tech refresh cycle	$10,000	$1,000	$9,000
Insurance & liability	$5,000	$200	$4,800
Total Annual Business Savings	—	—	**$74,800**

Common Objections – And How to Neutralize Them

Objection	Countermeasure
"Team cohesion suffers."	Weekly standups + quarterly in-persons + shared comms standards = restored culture.

"Harder to supervise performance."	Output-based metrics replace visibility. Better signal-to-noise ratio.
"Client impressions drop."	Maintain a small flex office or offer on-site days. Most clients don't care anymore.
"Security and compliance."	Issue laptops, enforce VPNs, add endpoint protection.
"Not everyone thrives at home."	True. Offer a stipend for coworking or library space. Focus on *fit*, not force.

Strategic Architect Rule

Return to office is often driven by trust gaps and legacy thinking—not performance logic.

You're not paid for commuting. You're paid for output.

Work from home is not soft. It's not a perk. It's not "the easy way."

It's a distributed operating system that unlocks output, retention, and resilience for employees AND employers alike.

Final Point

When done right, remote work reduces reactivity, increases clarity, and creates asymmetric gains on both sides of the payroll. Smart organizations are already reaping that advantage. Everyone else is just playing office until their employees vote with their feet and move to the organizations offering that flexibility.

Chapter 3: The ROI of Perfectionism

Perfection is waste unless failure is fatal.

Core Problem

For most tasks of average difficulty and scope, you can reach 80% completion in a few focused sessions. I have no sourcing on that except to say that average tasks require average inputs.

It's the final 20%—the polish, tweaks, and second guessing—where time, bandwidth, and momentum go to die.

You burn hours, days, even weeks chasing marginal gains only you will notice—and that your audience may not even value.

Perfectionism isn't precision. It's procrastination with better PR.

Strategic Architect Disclaimer – When 100% Is Worth It

Not every task can be optimized for speed. Some functions (emergency surgery, treaty language, or rocket trajectories) demand total precision. In those cases, the last 20% isn't waste. It's safety, legality, or structural integrity. And in a few select cases, that last 1% or even that last 0.001% are critical to mission success or sustaining human life. In edge-case systems—such as those tied to legality, physics, or mortality—the final decimal point is where the mission lives or dies.

However, put this on my tombstone:

Perfection is waste unless failure is fatal.

Strategic laziness doesn't mean cutting everything. It means knowing exactly what never gets cut. When failure has no margin, chase 100%. But most of what clogs your day doesn't fall into that category. You're not designing a pacemaker; you're replying to email.

This book isn't about cutting corners. It's about knowing which corners are cosmetic.

Systems / Tactics – How to Beat the Polishing Trap

Understand the time vs. quality curve:

- 0-80% – Steep, Efficient Gains: In this early phase, effort maps directly to results. Each unit of time invested delivers a noticeable improvement in perceived quality. This is the high-leverage zone, in which most of the value is created quickly.
- 80-95% – Slowing Returns, Rising Cost: Progress is still possible, but it costs more. The same amount of time yields smaller gains. You're polishing, refining, tightening. Useful, but no longer efficient.
- 95-100% – The Plateau: Every extra percentage point demands exponential effort. You're now fighting friction, not adding value. The work becomes obsessive, expensive, or performative. This is *Diminishing Returns Territory*, where perfectionism burns time with little to show for it.

Set 80% as the real goalpost:

- Ship it when it's *functional*, *clear*, and *usable*.
- Improve based on real-world friction, not imagined perfection.

Analogy – Cars and Returns

An **80% car** might lack heated seats, radar cruise control, or soft-close doors. A **100% car** adds $30,000 for details only a car reviewer cares about.

But if you need to get to work today, and you're on a budget, the 80% car wins every time.

The same goes for work, writing, strategy, and systems. The same thing goes for this book!

Apply the market lens by asking:
- Will the target user notice the last 20% of polish?
- Will they pay more because of it?
- Will it change adoption?

If not, you're polishing for your own pride, not for impact.

Strategic Architect Rule

Use version control. Label every major effort by version:
- V0 = Draft
- V1 = Ready for field use
- V2 = Polished
- V3 = Polished again *if* there's ROI

V1 ships. V2 improves. V3 is optional. Don't wait for a mythical "final form." Real feedback is better than guesswork in a vacuum.

Tactics to Escape Perfection Paralysis

- **Timebox high-fidelity work.** Set a cap. Then ship.
- **Declare "good enough" publicly.** Make accountability external.
- **Accept certain visible imperfections.** Most users never notice. The smart ones respect your speed.
- **Use the 24-hour Rule.** Done by end-of-day, not end-of-doubt.

ROI Table – Output by Effort Band

Effort Level	Time Invested (Relative)	Perceived Quality Gain	Relative ROI
V0: First Draft (0–60%)	20%	65%	High
V1: Functional Product (60–80%)	30%	25%	High
V2: Polished Work (80–95%)	30%	7%	Moderate
V3: Final Polish (95–99.9%)	20%	1–3%	Low

Closing Thought

An 80% product today usually beats a 99% product next month. A shipped version always outperforms the perfect draft in Google Drive.

Done and room to learn scales. Perfect and stuck dies.

Chapter 4: Scaling Solo – System Design Without a Team

You don't need more people. You need better systems.

Core Problem

Solo operators can get stuck. Not because they lack motivation, but because they try to scale through *effort* instead of *architecture*.

You don't scale by doing more. You scale by building systems that don't need you to do everything. If you're a solopreneur, startup lead, side hustler, or project owner, your job isn't just to execute. It's to design a repeatable engine that multiplies your output without multiplying your time input.

Strategic Architect Rule

If you're doing it more than once, systemize it. If it takes more than 15 minutes, make it modular. If it still needs you after a week, fix the architecture.

Core Systems for Scaling Without Staff

1. **Prebuilt Responses and Outreach Templates**
   - Common questions, sales follow-ups, vendor negotiations
   - Store them. Iterate. Reuse.
2. **Asynchronous Work Blocks**
   - Don't sync live unless you must.
   - Record instructions.
   - Set deadlines.
   - Push documents, not meetings.
3. **Minimum Viable Launch Systems**
   - You don't need a perfect funnel. You need a Stripe link and a clear offer.
4. **Cognitive Offloading Systems**
   - Use apps, not your brain, to track status, steps, and files.
   - If you forget a task, the system failed. Not you.
5. **"Default Off" Channels**
   - Close inbox tabs. Disable real-time alerts.
   - Check communication like you check the mail: on schedule, not impulse.
6. **Daily ELI (Effort, Leverage, Impact) Prioritization**

- If you're burned out, you're probably prioritizing high-effort, low-impact work. Kill it or delay it.

Solo ROI Table – Systems That Buy Back Your Time

Subtraction System	Weekly Hours Saved	Annual Hours Saved	Annual Value	Lifetime Value
Default templates (inquiries, outreach, scheduling)	2	104	$5,200	$260,000
Modular task framework (Standard Operating Procedures)	1.5	78	$3,900	$195,000
Asynchronous work protocols	2	104	$5,200	$260,000

Summary
Working alone is not a weakness. It's a constraint. And constraints are where real system builders thrive. You don't need a team to build scale. You just need systems that act like one.

Chapter 5: Half the Time, All the Value

You don't have to do it every day. That's the myth that kills momentum. People hear "Subtraction System" and assume they need to flip their lives upside down.

No.

You just need to do it **half the time.**

Stop making your bed three days a week. You save 4-6 hours a year. Bring lunch from home twice a week. You save $1,000 a year. Skip just one 30-minute meeting per week. That's 26 hours back to you each year.

The ROI is still exponential, and you have more than recouped your investment in this book.

Subtraction isn't binary. It compounds.

Every rep you run, every shortcut you keep, every system you deploy—even at 50% fidelity—pays you. Not in theory. In minutes, hours, dollars, and cognitive clarity.
It doesn't have to be clean. It doesn't have to be pretty. It just has to start.

Subtraction Systems are friction sensitive. The more you use them, the more they integrate. But to see the return, you don't need a five-year plan. You need a Tuesday.

And here's the kicker: Once you see the time and money come back, once you feel the bandwidth open up, you'll want more. That's the engine. Not discipline. Not willpower. It's ROI.

You're not optimizing your life. You're optimizing the cost of delay. If a system costs you three minutes to set up but gives you back 30, doing it half the time is still a 5x return.

But no system is bulletproof; learn what to do when subtraction backfires.

Chapter 6: Subtraction Doctrine – Failure Mode Protocols

Misapplied systems can:
- Over-optimize and create brittleness
- Kill high-ROI items by accident
- Undermine trust, joy, or health in pursuit of "efficiency"
- Be misapplied by someone who doesn't understand the underlying architecture

This is your recovery protocol, the one you activate when a Subtraction System starts creating friction instead of reducing it. When you deleted something that looked inefficient, but had been doing invisible work.

If you make a mistake and subtract the wrong thing, here is how you come back from it.

Strategic Architect Rule
Every system has a failure mode. Smart systems plan for it. Great systems evolve from it. Subtraction Systems are a strategic weapon, cutting friction to reclaim leverage. But even weapons can misfire.

Examples:
- Canceling a weekly sync that also served as a morale check
- Automating a human reply that used to build trust
- Eliminating a task that felt like a time sink, but actually kept you grounded

System Recovery:
- Re-run the ROI math. Include indirect value: trust, morale, presence
- If the gain is abstract, build a replacement explicitly (e.g., morale tracking, trust sync)
- Ask: What problem did this solve before I cut it?

Author's Note: Not all ROI is visible on a spreadsheet. Especially when humans are involved. You try to automate before the task is stable. You delete before the replacement is battle-tested.

Examples:
- Auto-scheduling before you've verified availability
- Delegating a task that requires judgment you haven't taught
- Killing a habit before the replacement is sticky

System Recovery:
- Install a two-step rule: no automation without prior observation
- Track system stability for one to two weeks before full subtraction
- Keep a V1/V2 distinction: "functional" before "optimized"

Strategic Architect Rule
Suppose you build an enviable system, and someone copies it. Poorly. Now it's being misused and of course, your name is on it.

Examples:

- A teammate steals your template system and applies it to sensitive messaging
- A boss sees your calendar audit and applies the 1/3-2/3 rule with zero context
- Someone weaponizes your "don't make your bed" rule in a leadership forum

System Recovery:
- Add context guards: "This only works if x, y, z are true"
- Build "failure case" examples into your documentation
- If needed, disavow and document: blame James.

Strategic Architect Rule

A system that started sharp can become bloated, misaligned, or redundant. But it remains active if no one challenges it. Constantly audit your systems.

Examples:
- Your half-hour Sunday reset becomes a three-hour checklist of low-impact rituals
- Your pre-pack system has ten "essentials" you never use
- Your workflow has six redundant steps, all leftovers from earlier versions

System Recovery:
- Quarterly kill review: what's no longer needed?
- Recalculate the ROI math
- Replace "just in case" with "when was it last used?"

Field Note: Effective systems include operating instructions and warnings. Don't start treating everything like a spreadsheet and forget that life is lived in the white space.

Examples:
- You cut the bedtime routine because it's "inefficient," and your kid pulls away
- You stop taking long walks because they don't "optimize cardio output," and lose clarity
- You standardize meals and forget you liked cooking

System Recovery:
- Run an audit: which subtractions made your life worse?
- Reinstate or reimagine them. Joy is ROI.
- Use "strategic inefficiencies" deliberately. Name them. Protect them.

If it costs time but restores energy, it's not really a leak. It's a refuel.

Execution Note: Every system becomes drag if you never subtract from it.

You assume $50/hour and 260-day years are eternal.

Examples:
- You change jobs, and your effective time value triples
- You retire, and realize many systems no longer save you anything
- You re-read the book in 2040, and the math doesn't track

System Recovery:
- **Step 1: New hourly rate**
  New rate = total income / total active hours
  (Not just work hours; include commute, email, stress carryover)
- **Step 2: New activity grid**
  Use real-world logs: which days are full bandwidth? Which aren't?
- **Step 3: Recalculate value**
  ROI = minutes saved $\times$ days used $\times$ new hourly rate $\div$ 60

You don't need a new book. You need new inputs.

Strategic Architect Rule

Every number is an assumption. Strong systems let you swap the variables. A bad system teaches. A failed system clarifies. A misused system makes the case for a better one. You're not here to follow the rules. You're here to evolve them. And now, your doctrine evolves too.

Chapter 7: The Multiplier Effect

We've spent this book in the weeds—killing chores, retooling routines, upgrading how you move, think, eat, and lead. But Subtraction Systems don't just change your day. If adopted at scale, they change the world.

That's right, I'm going to entertain some delusions of grandeur right now and posit that Subtraction Systems can help the world optimize, provide more time for everyone, and lead us into a new age of efficiency. A guy can dream, no?

This isn't utopian. It's math.

If one person saves 30 minutes a day, they reclaim 182 hours a year. That's four and a half work weeks.

If a team of 20 saves the same, it's 3,640 hours—nearly two full-time employees' worth of bandwidth.

Now scale that to an agency. A county, a state, or a country. How about a global workforce bleeding time on low-value work, reactive communication, duplicated effort, and bureaucratic drag?

Subtraction Systems are the antidote to systemic inefficiency. They're not hacks. They're architecture. And architecture, when replicated, becomes infrastructure.

This is what happened with the démarche redesign. What saved me five minutes saved the system more than 9,000 hours a year. That's the power of designing once and scaling forever. Look at how the U.S. Army saved a billion dollars a year and millions of man-hours by ditching two stupid rituals, and hardly anyone noticed.

And it's not just about time. It's about cognition. Every hour you get back is an hour not spent drowning in email, rewriting the same briefing, or reacting to noise. And once you clear that space? You can think. You can solve. You can build.

Systems move missions. Systems build leverage. And systems at scale move nations.

That's the real play here. Not inbox zero. Not white-glove uniform inspections.

The endgame is to free up enough attention, at enough altitude, to solve real problems.
No one's coming to save us from inefficiency. But we don't need salvation. We need design.

We need Strategic Architects.

90-Day Systems Check-In

Every system drifts. This checkpoint helps you realign. What's working? What's cluttered? What's costing more than it returns? Don't just review results; review architecture. Good systems compound. Bad ones calcify.

After three months, it's time to reflect. Which Subtraction Systems worked? Which failed? Why?

- Which systems are still active?
- Which systems surprised you by how well they worked?
- Where are you still losing time, money or energy?
- What did you try to implement but gave up on?
- What new systems did you build or adapt on your own?
- Which ones are still running clean, and which ones need to be burned down or rebuilt?

Revisit the diagnostic. Re-score your systems. Bandwidth is a cycle; keep subtracting.

After you'd had some time to audit your systems, take the test on the next page.

Rate each item as 1 (Yes) or 0 (No). Only count it if it's active, repeatable, and saves you time. At the end, total your score and check your status.

The Final Exam: Do You Think Like a Strategic Architect?

#	Subtraction System	Yes (1) / No (0)
SECTION I: Strategic Foundations		
1	I start tasks when they can run without me ("Start Necessary Movement")	
2	I calculate ROI on time before committing to habits or systems	
3	I use planning tools like Troop Leading Procedures (TLPs) to reverse-plan deliverables	
4	I identify and follow desire paths instead of using brute-force effort	
5	I apply the Strategic Architect lens to system design	
SECTION II: Work Like a Weapon		
6	I use the T/C/S format (Task/Condition/Standard) when assigning tasks	
7	I reduce email load with templates, canned responses, and group my inbox by threads	
8	I batch messages and turn off real-time alerts	
9	I limit meetings to agenda-based or asynchronous formats	
10	I apply the 1/3 Planning, 2/3 Execution rule to protect deep work blocks	
11	I use hotkeys to eliminate precise mouse movements and clicks	
12	I delegate using authority, automation, or logic	
13	My team runs independently due to supervision systems (backbriefs)	
14	I align outputs with approval systems	
SECTION III: First Routines		
15	My morning routine omits unnecessary decisions and prep	
16	I wear decision-free clothing and use prepositioned gear	
17	I use slip-on shoes or fast-transition gear	
18	I pre-pack my bag and prep items the night before	
19	I combine hygiene tasks (e.g. shave + shower)	
20	I skip ironing, folding, bed-making, tie-tying, toothpaste top-unscrewing	
21	I use visual systems (externalized, kid-friendly tools that replace verbal reminders with visual cues) for kid routines	
SECTION IV: Home Base		
22	I've automated or delegated recurring chores	
23	I use shared lists and/or repeat orders for groceries	
24	I've optimized appliance ROI (robot vac, dehumidifier, etc.)	

25	I've created elder/childcare plans that reduce daily drag	
26	My family can function without me for at least 24 hours	
27	I keep pre-packed go bags ready for common situations	
SECTION V: Subtract to Learn		
28	I eat a default breakfast and/or lunch to reduce decisions	
29	I batch or modularize dinner prep	
30	I use time-saving cooking tools (e.g. air fryer)	
31	I've solved hydration with a go-to system	
32	I rarely snack reactively due to consistent food routines	
33	I help cognitive load with passive (i.e. audiobooks) and retrieval-based learning (i.e. summarizing from memory)	
34	I skip ads and adjust playback speed to compress learning	
SECTION VI: Work by Design		
35	I walk, run, or bike to work to repurpose commute time	
36	I've eliminated or minimized my commute	
37	I work from home with a structured, repeatable system	
38	I use block scheduling to shape my workday	
39	I design time blocks intentionally (not all time is fungible)	
40	I preserve slack time for family, emergencies, or resets	

Score: _____ / 40

Archetype Scoring

Score Range	Title	Interpretation
0–10	The Grinder	Running on effort, not systems. Start subtracting.
11–20	The Overleveraged	Fragments of structure, but drag still dominates.
21–30	The Architect-in-Training	Gaining leverage, but there's still clutter.
31–37	The High-Leverager	A fine-tuned system, with just a few friction points left.
38+	Strategic Architect	You've deleted almost every nonessential drag vector. The system runs without you.

Epilogue: What…Would You Say…You Do Here?

The systems in this book will give you back hundreds of hours per year. The question is: what will you do with them?

Some people use their reclaimed time to train. Some to rest. Some to finally start the thing they've been putting off.

Time isn't money. Time is where money, relationships, clarity, and impact all start. You already have the time. This book just returns it to you.

What you do with it is up to you.

Subtraction Systems by Difficulty and ROI

Subtraction System	Days per Year	Minutes Saved Daily	Hours Saved Yearly	Days Saved Lifetime	Annual Value	Lifetime Value	Difficulty	ROI
Fliptop toothpaste	365	0.1	1	1	$30	$1,521	2	1
Belt (ratchet-style, fast adjust)	260	0.3	1	2	$54	$2,708	2	1
Avoided baggage fees (2x a year)	365	-	-	-	$75	$3,750	1	1
Late fees / overdrafts avoided	365	-	-	-	$100	$5,000	1	1
Badge/lanyard (ready & reachable)	260	1	2	5	$108	$5,417	2	1
News audit	260	1	2	5	$108	$5,417	2	1
Origin story & intro prep	260	1	2	5	$108	$5,417	2	1
Medical binder (20-year cap)	365	1	6	13	$304	$6,083	2	1
Legal/doc storage (20-year cap)	365	1	6	13	$304	$6,083	2	1
Scheduled check-ins (20-year cap)	365	1	6	13	$304	$6,083	2	1
Standard scripts/templates (20-year cap)	365	1	6	13	$304	$6,083	2	1
Coordination time avoided (20-year cap)	365	1	6	13	$304	$6,083	2	1
Escalator discipline	365	1	3	6	$152	$7,604	2	1
Subscription audit savings	365	-	-	-	$200	$10,000	1	1
Slip-on tie	260	1	4	9	$217	$10,833	2	2
Shoes (pre-tied or slip-on)	260	1	4	9	$217	$10,833	2	2
Shoehorn use (speed + no bending)	260	1	4	9	$217	$10,833	2	2
Pre-packed laptop bag	260	1	4	9	$217	$10,833	2	2
Reusable shopping bags	260	1	4	9	$217	$10,833	2	2
Rechargeable-only systems	260	1	4	9	$217	$10,833	2	2
Weekly frag-day audit	52	5	4	9	$217	$10,833	2	2
Swipe file + reuse	260	1	5	11	$260	$13,000	2	2
No checked baggage	365	1	6	13	$304	$15,208	2	2
Packing/unpacking time saved	365	1	6	13	$304	$15,208	2	2
Skipping bed-making	365	1	6	13	$304	$15,208	2	2
Standardized grooming kit	365	1	6	13	$304	$15,208	2	2
Reusable water bottle	365	1	6	13	$304	$15,208	2	2
Shared household list	365	1	6	13	$304	$15,208	2	2
Doorway/hall blocking	365	1	6	13	$304	$15,208	2	2
Crosswalk awareness	365	1	6	13	$304	$15,208	2	2
Trail efficiency	365	1	6	13	$304	$15,208	2	2
Cycling shortcut logic	365	1	6	13	$304	$15,208	2	2
Line-readiness + public prep	365	1	6	13	$304	$15,208	2	2
Noise & space etiquette	365	1	6	13	$304	$15,208	2	2
Pre-packed go bag	365	1	6	13	$304	$15,208	2	2
Function-based packing	365	1	6	13	$304	$15,208	2	2

Subtraction System	Days per Year	Minutes Saved Daily	Hours Saved Yearly	Days Saved Lifetime	Annual Value	Lifetime Value	Difficulty	ROI
Setup zone system (deployment)	365	1	6	13	$304	$15,208	2	2
Reduced forgotten items	365	1	6	13	$304	$15,208	2	2
"Leave the House" drill	365	1	6	13	$304	$15,208	2	2
Shower + Mouthwash + Pee	365	1	6	13	$304	$15,208	2	2
No ironing / outfit changes	365	1	6	13	$304	$15,208	2	2
Reduce suit dry cleaning (23 fewer × $15)	-	-	-	-	$345	$17,250	1	2
Eliminating color separation in laundry	365	1	9	18	$426	$21,292	2	2
Quiet kit (saves reschedules)	365	1	9	18	$426	$21,292	2	2
Email filters + auto-archive	260	2	9	19	$455	$22,750	2	2
Eliminate shirt dry cleaning (156 × $3)	-	-	-	-	$468	$23,400	1	2
Prebuilt slide decks + 1-pagers	260	2	10	21	$498	$24,917	2	2
Cost avoided (bottled water)	365	-	-	-	$520	$26,000	1	2
No-fold policy (socks/underwear)	365	2	12	25	$608	$30,417	2	2
Shave + Shower	365	2	12	25	$608	$30,417	2	2
Scheduling links	260	3	13	26	$628	$31,417	2	2
Batch laundry (vs. daily)	365	2	13	27	$639	$31,938	2	2
Coffee Maker	365	2	13	27	$639	$31,938	2	2
Notification shutdown	260	3	13	27	$650	$32,500	2	2
Boilerplate shortcuts	260	3	13	27	$650	$32,500	2	2
Pre-packed kits	365	2	14	29	$700	$34,979	2	2
Iron-free shirt system	365	3	18	38	$913	$45,625	2	2
Washer/Dryer (no clothes sorting)	365	3	18	38	$913	$45,625	2	2
Visual systems for kids	365	3	18	38	$913	$45,625	2	2
Manual bill pay eliminated	365	3	18	38	$913	$45,625	2	2
Reduced stress / distraction time	365	3	18	38	$913	$45,625	2	2
ChatGPT task automation	260	4	19	39	$932	$46,583	2	2
Templates for writing/speaking	260	5	20	42	$997	$49,833	2	2
Childcare logistics buffer (10-year cap)	260	12	50	104	$2,492	$49,833	3	2
Default meal system	365	4	21	44	$1,065	$53,229	2	3
Email templates & canned replies	260	5	22	45	$1,083	$54,167	2	3
Messaging app batching	260	5	22	45	$1,083	$54,167	2	3
1/3–2/3 scheduling rule	260	5	22	45	$1,083	$54,167	2	3
Burnout breaks (prevented)	260	5	22	45	$1,083	$54,167	2	3
Default daypack loadout	260	5	22	45	$1,083	$54,167	2	3
Slip-on gear (tie, belt, shoes)	260	5	22	45	$1,083	$54,167	2	3
Decision-proof footwear	260	5	22	45	$1,083	$54,167	2	3
Focus/Do Not Disturb use	260	5	22	45	$1,083	$54,167	2	3
Core hotkeys (Word/Excel)	260	5	22	45	$1,083	$54,167	2	3

Subtraction System	Days per Year	Minutes Saved Daily	Hours Saved Yearly	Days Saved Lifetime	Annual Value	Lifetime Value	Difficulty	ROI
Command stringing / macros	260	5	22	45	$1,083	$54,167	2	3
Wardrobe/logistics prep	260	5	22	45	$1,083	$54,167	2	3
Appearance management	260	5	22	45	$1,083	$54,167	2	3
5-minute backbriefs (daily tasks)	260	5	22	45	$1,083	$54,167	2	3
Autonomy systems (less checking)	260	5	22	45	$1,083	$54,167	2	3
Error reduction (via T/C/S clarity)	260	5	22	45	$1,083	$54,167	2	3
Fewer unnecessary meetings	260	5	22	45	$1,083	$54,167	2	3
Fewer dry cleaner trips (48 fewer x 30 min)	260	6	24	51	$1,213	$60,667	3	3
Dishwasher (no pre-wash)	365	4	24	51	$1,217	$60,833	2	3
Batching errands	365	4	24	51	$1,217	$60,833	2	3
Default breakfast	365	4	24	51	$1,217	$60,833	2	3
Lunch system (3x/week)	365	4	24	51	$1,217	$60,833	2	3
Modular meal prep	365	4	24	51	$1,217	$60,833	2	3
Speed + ad skip + pairing logic	260	6	25	52	$1,257	$62,833	3	3
Readwise → Notion review loop	260	6	25	52	$1,257	$62,833	3	3
Up/Down Chain Integrity	260	6	26	54	$1,300	$65,000	3	3
Cancel recurring meetings	260	6	26	54	$1,300	$65,000	3	3
Async updates vs. live syncs	260	6	26	54	$1,300	$65,000	3	3
15-minute default duration	260	6	26	54	$1,300	$65,000	3	3
Grocery pickup/delivery	365	4	26	54	$1,308	$65,396	2	3
Night-before prep	365	4	26	54	$1,308	$65,396	2	3
Delegated chores	365	5	28	58	$1,399	$69,958	2	3
Dehumidifier drain hose fix (2x day)	365	5	30	63	$1,521	$76,042	2	3
Morning ramp-up (friction reduction)	365	5	30	63	$1,521	$76,042	2	3
Evening shutdown (better prep & sleep)	365	5	30	63	$1,521	$76,042	2	3
Smart Cookers (air fryer, etc.)	365	5	30	63	$1,521	$76,042	2	3
Auto-deliveries (basics)	365	5	30	63	$1,521	$76,042	2	3
Calendar + Sunday Sync	365	5	30	63	$1,521	$76,042	2	3
Better sleep quality	365	5	30	63	$1,521	$76,042	2	3
Fixed inbox check windows	260	8	33	68	$1,625	$81,250	3	3
Audio learning at drop-off	230	10	38	80	$1,917	$95,833	3	3
Task Clarity (T/C/S format)	260	9	39	81	$1,950	$97,500	3	3
Email batching	260	9	39	81	$1,950	$97,500	3	3
Social media controls	260	10	43	90	$2,167	$108,333	3	3
Passive learning (podcasts/audio)	260	10	43	90	$2,167	$108,333	3	3
Decompression/re-ramp time	260	10	43	90	$2,167	$108,333	3	3
Wardrobe/logistics drag	260	10	43	90	$2,167	$108,333	3	3
Meals + coffee logistics	260	10	43	90	$2,167	$108,333	3	3

Subtraction System	Days per Year	Minutes Saved Daily	Hours Saved Yearly	Days Saved Lifetime	Annual Value	Lifetime Value	Difficulty	ROI
Decompression/re-ramp buffer	260	10	43	90	$2,167	$108,333	3	3
Directive Communication	260	12	52	108	$2,600	$130,000	3	4
Delegation with Ownership	260	12	52	108	$2,600	$130,000	3	4
Robot vacuum	365	9	52	109	$2,616	$130,792	3	4
Outsourced chores	365	9	56	117	$2,798	$139,917	3	4
Parallel routines	365	10	61	127	$3,042	$152,083	3	4
Workout audio learning	260	15	65	135	$3,250	$162,500	3	4
Commute audio learning	260	30	130	271	$6,500	$325,000	2	5
Commute eliminated (1hr/day)	260	60	260	542	$13,000	$650,000	5	5
Run commute (10k)	130	varies	varies	varies	varies	varies	5	5
Bike commute (20k)	130	varies	varies	varies	varies	varies	5	5
Walk commute (3.2k)	130	varies	varies	varies	varies	varies	5	5
Totals	--	546	2,609	5,436	######	$6,488,233	--	--

Subtraction System Difficulty Key

Tier	Difficulty	Definition
1	None	You stop doing something and gain time immediately. No action required.
2	Minimal	A small, one-time setup or habit tweak (e.g. moving your coffeepot, purchasing slip-on shoes).
3	Moderate	A recurring change that requires modest effort or consistency (e.g., pre-packing gear, night-before prep).
4	Hard	Requires real behavioral change, coordination with others, or multiple steps (e.g. systemizing chores, delegating work).
5	Extreme	High friction or prolonged setup. Deep change to routines, mindsets, or environments (e.g., designing scalable work systems, launching automation tools).

Subtraction System ROI Key

Tier	ROI	Lifetime Value Range	Days Saved Lifetime (Approx)	Example Systems
1	Minimal	$0 – $10,000	0–20 days	Fliptop toothpaste, no baggage, subscription audit

2	Moderate	$10,001 – $50,000	20–50 days	No-fold laundry, reusable water bottle, email templates
3	High	$50,001 – $125,000	50–100 days	Night-before prep, ChatGPT tasking, batching, default meals
4	Major	$125,001 – $300,000	100–200 days	Parallel routines, audio learning, delegation w/ownership
5	Extreme	$300,001+	200+ days	Commute eliminated, robot vacuum + passive learning stack

GLOSSARY

Term	Definition in This Book
1/3–2/3 rule	A military and time management guideline positing that leaders should spend one-third of the mission's allocated time on planning, and the other two-thirds on execution.
Backbrief	A rapid, verbal confirmation of understanding. Used to close out tasking: "What's your next step?" "What will you do if x happens?" It replaces check-ins with clarity.
Bandwidth	Usable surplus of time, energy, money, and/or mental clarity. Not leisure or luxury. Bandwidth is operational slack: what you buy back when you remove friction.
Bandwidth Stacking	Compounding multiple efficiencies in one action. Example: running while listening to a podcast and minding a toddler. Three wins in one block of time.
Burnout Break	A pre-scheduled day of zero output, built to protect the system. Taken before collapse, not after.
Calendar Audit	A systematic review of calendar entries to eliminate low-ROI commitments and enforce intentional time use. Often the first Subtraction System.
Command Stringing	Combining multiple keyboard hotkeys or system actions into one continuous motion. Saves time and movement.
Commander's Intent	A clear and concise expression of the purpose of the operation and the desired end state that supports mission command, provides focus to the staff, and helps subordinate and supporting commanders act to achieve the commander's desired results without further orders.
Decision Drag	Mental friction caused by too many choices. Default systems eliminate this. Example: same breakfast every day = no morning deliberation.
Decision-Free Clothing	Preselected outfits that eliminate micro-decisions and streamline daily prep.
Dehumidifier Doctrine	An illustrative metaphor for low-attention, high-return systems, like a dehumidifier that runs silently but improves the entire space.
Delegation Modes	The three primary types of offloading: **Authority** (human delegation), **Mechanical** (tool-driven), and **Ownership Enforcement** (requiring minimal future inputs).
Desire Path	The frictionless route people actually take, even when it deviates from the "official" one. In this book, systems are designed desire paths: shortcuts that stick.
ELI Score	A matrix for prioritizing tasks based on **Effort**, **Leverage**, and **Impact**. Higher scores indicate high-value Subtraction Systems.

Flow	A state of deliberate, low-resistance execution. Unlike the psychological concept of "flow state," here it refers to clean, uninterrupted systems movement, e.g. morning routines, workflow, awareness in public spaces.
Frag Days	Days that appear open but are structurally compromised (travel, kid duty, off-site, holidays). Require special planning to preserve bandwidth.
Frag Order	An operational order issued for the purpose of adjusting a previous order; it is an expedient means of communicating critical plan modifications to units, particularly when time is in short supply or situations are rapidly evolving.
Friction	Any unnecessary delay, decision, or cognitive tax that wastes bandwidth.
Grind Mode	Default operating state for many people. Characterized by fatigue, low strategic thinking, and unnecessary effort. Often worn like a badge of honor.
Grinder	Someone who works constantly but inefficiently, relying on effort over systems. They get results, but at too high a cost in time and energy.
Pre-loaded	Already built and ready for immediate use. Pre-packed bags, templated emails, default settings; anything that doesn't require startup effort.
Signal	Useful information, clear feedback, real needs, or actionable truth. It's what's left when you subtract noise. Your systems should be designed to surface signal faster, and ignore everything else.
Slack Time	Pre-reserved, unscheduled time blocks used to handle the unexpected without disrupting essential priorities.
Strategic Architect	A person who intentionally designs systems that scale, stack, and sustain performance across domains. Not reactive; constructive.
Subtraction System	Any process, habit, or decision framework designed to reduce drag, eliminate unnecessary inputs, or reclaim time, money, or cognitive bandwidth. Subtraction Systems often appear mundane but deliver compounding benefits.
System	A repeatable structure that reduces decision fatigue and increases output. Not necessarily tech or software; a system is anything you do more than once that you've streamlined.
System Stack	The idea that Subtraction Systems unlock or reinforce one another. For example, inbox batching creates the space for deep work, which in turn enables effective delegation.
T/C/S Format	Task/Condition/Standard. A framework for giving clear, measurable instructions. Borrowed from military doctrine but repurposed for high-leverage civilian work.
TLPs	Troop Leading Procedures. A step-by-step sequential process military leaders use to plan, coordinate, make decisions, and conduct operations.
Weaponized Friction	A satirical take on how to introduce inefficiencies into others' systems, illustrating the real cost of micro-friction.

| **Work by Design** | A philosophy that argues the best systems work not just harder, but differently, designed once to scale many. Contrast with grind culture. |